The Constitution of Government

in Galt's Gulch

Dedicated to the courageous men and women
of Law Enforcement and National Defense

Wolf DeVoon

ISBN 978-1499550450

CONTENTS

Preface

➤ GALT'S GULCH

➤ LIBERTY

➤ PROPERTY

(continued)

(continued)

➤ CONSTITUTIONAL LAW

➤ NATIONAL DEFENSE

PREFACE

Wolf DeVoon is an interesting character even by anarcho-libertarian standards. He is equal parts scholar and activist. Wolf is also a free man in both theory and in practice, which is very rare. Unlike many scholars of the anarcho-libertarian movement, he has eschewed a safe and easy sinecure at a webzine, think-tank, or a position on a university faculty. Instead Wolf has written, experienced, succeeded and failed at trying to move the concept and practice of individual liberty from the treatises and novels and into the actual world. For all his efforts, I am personally very grateful.

– Ali Hassan Massoud

A wannabe lawyer who places himself alongside some literary giants is a fascinating study in ego pathology. There has to be name for this disease but I can't stop laughing long enough to look it up.

– Simon Jester

Most men hope to be celebrated and successful, remembered for achievements that made life easier for others. That was never my purpose. I selfishly sought knowledge and seized opportunities when offered. I repeatedly made life more difficult for others.

Tibor Machan once shouted at me: "It's important to be right!" to which I replied "It's more important to be original."

I still believe that to be true. Children stand in the fire hose of good evidence and philosophically well formed formulas, unable to resist, unless someone takes a hatchet to the damn thing and says: Wait a minute, let me think for myself.

Wolf DeVoon

Galt's Gulch

in theory and
practical experience

Who is John Galt?

Dagny crashes an airplane and all is revealed. John Galt is handsome, brilliant, virile, cheerful, tender, implacable and chaste. Everyone in the Gulch obeys him immediately and willingly. The only thing Galt wants (and can't have) is Dagny.

Fiction enjoys the privilege of projecting an ideal, a marriage made in heaven, so to speak, with best man Francisco and second-best Hank proudly acquiescing to the inevitable destiny of Galt winning Dagny whereupon everyone lives happily ever after. Francisco probably found another babe to impress with quadratic equations, and Hank's heroism was rewarded by reunion with Gwen Ives?

It's unclear in my mind whether I read Atlas first, or Fountainhead, but Roark made a far greater impression on me than Galt. Thinking back, I must have read Atlas first, which I found stuck behind an old cabinet in my girlfriend's shared apartment, left there by a previous tenant. It so profoundly changed my outlook on life that I refused to open Fountainhead, unwilling to tarnish the shining vistas of Atlas, until artist Tom Alexander recommended I read it. I found it difficult to discount anything Tom said, because he trumped me in moral philosophy. A shy, silent recluse who stuttered, Tom allowed me to see his paintings. They were astoundingly good. The very canvas throbbed with living power, and I said so — which angered Tom to blurt in frustration: "F-f-f-fl-flattery is b-b-b-b-bullshit!"

So I read Fountainhead because Tom said it was important and, sure enough, Tom was right. To this day I regard Fountainhead as Rand's best work of fiction.

What was it that made Roark more important to me than Galt?

Roark was disgraced, penniless and powerless. The only thing Roark could do was refuse to compromise, which echoed my own plight.

John Galt, on the other hand, commanded limitless power from an invention that no one else understands because it's a macguffin. He has a chat with two of his college buddies and Midas, and presto! — the United States government falls and hundreds of thousands if not millions of innocent women and children starve to death.

The business of starving people to death is a sore point with liberals and likewise the reason that conservatives kept their mouths shut when Atlas appeared in 1957. No one was willing to speak in favor of it. Personally, starving doesn't bother me. I've been there, done that, more than once.

What bothers me is Galt as I described him at the beginning of this chapter: handsome, brilliant, virile, cheerful, tender, implacable and chaste — in other words, everything I'm not and never could be. The last thing anyone will applaud me for is chastity, and in previous writing I confessed to having a second-class brain.

> *I am painfully aware of apparent individuality and diversity, six billion unique lifestyles and hairstyles and nicknames. That's not the problem. The problem is that no one truly wishes to be who they are. I had hoped for a life like David Lean or Stanley Kubrick. In a pinch, I would have settled for Fred Zinneman. What I got instead was Wolf DeVoon -- an isolated beatnik with a second-class brain, whose idea of a good time is a newspaper and a cup of coffee at Denny's.*

I don't believe in hiding the truth. It is difficult enough to speak as simply as possible, without having to memorize a pack of lies. Rand's achievement in Atlas Shrugged was superlative. More importantly, her Introduction to Objectivist Epistemology is a high springboard from which future generations of philosophers will attempt the somersault of validating natural language to rescue predicate logic. I wish them swift success on that urgent mission.

But the remaining work of Objectivism will be most likely done by ugly, awkward, paranoid, callous, mercurial misfits, not unlike Rand herself who was not John Galt.

Which brings us to a rather sad fact. There was no John Galt in 1957, there is no John Galt among us today, and there cannot be a John Galt in the future.

Galt's fictional achievements in physics and moral suasion resemble an amalgam of Albert Einstein, Obi-Wan Kanobi, and Jimmy Stewart.

His crusade to 'destroy' the best and brightest did not happen in 1957 and it wouldn't get past a TSA departure gate or EPA Region 8 today. The future is going to be worse, not better, in terms of government surveillance and privacy. There isn't a square centimeter of Colorado in which to hide behind a heated layer of air. Industry is something that happens in China and South Korea, not Pennsylvania or Ohio.

I'm agreeable to the notion of genius. In previous writing I predicted

> *A single genius can and will compel the world to something better than liberal democracy, defining a wider and deeper conception of liberty.*

But it won't be wise old Judge Narragansett crossing out delegated powers and adding new language. A written constitution, no matter how brilliantly conceived and crafted, cannot ratify or enforce itself.

The Gulch in Fiction

I'm doing this from memory, without checking the text of Atlas, so please laugh if I get something wrong. Midas lives in Chicago, but he decides to buy a big chunk of Colorado, an entire mountain valley and two or three sections on either side. Who did Midas buy it from? Which county recorded the deed? How did he build a house without hiring a construction crew who arrived by road? Okay, maybe they dynamited the road after building a house, a septic tank, and an air strip. Everyone was sworn to secrecy — long before Galt persuaded Midas to close his bank and subdivide the secret valley in Colorado that no federal, state, or county official knew anything about. Maybe there was a convenient bonfire at the county courthouse and the plat maps and deeds were destroyed. Nobody knows anything about the valley except Midas and a pilot who can find it VFR.

To have any sort of community, there has to be infrastructure. At a minimum, they need water. Okay, maybe the valley has a creek that could be dammed high enough to create a reservoir. That implies concrete construction, because sticks and stones wouldn't survive the first winter. The spring melt is a torrent. Okay, Midas is a genius. He anticipated community development and the construction crew who was sworn to secrecy built a dam and a sluice and did some grading before they went home and erased all evidence of road access. Later on when it became Galt's Gulch, someone flew in everything needed to distribute water and power (pipe, wire, transformers, condensers), Midas' car, foundry tools, steel tanks, light bulbs, kitchen stoves and plate glass. Nobody had to order any of this stuff from a factory or a distributor. No one saw it loaded on a cargo plane to be air dropped after clearing 12,000-ft peaks on oxygen. It all parachuted perfectly into the valley drop zone without mishap, and all the air crews were sworn to secrecy. Nobody ever blabbed about what was happening in Galt's Gulch and there were no forest rangers or neighbors.

The Gulch in Reality

For the moment, let's continue to call him Midas, except he's not a banker. He's a charismatic rogue appointed by a secretive team of heavy hitters who are fed up paying taxes, mostly Americans with a few Russians thrown in to make life interesting. They pony up $10 million to lease 10 square miles from Peru for 99 years to build a new Hong Kong called "Laissez Faire City." This almost succeeds, except that Alberto Fujimori is nervous about being prosecuted for crimes against humanity and $3 million in graft vanishes. **No 99-year lease.**

Enter John Galt, a respected Wharton economist and tech guru, who proposes to implement Laissez Faire City in cyberspace with strong encryption. You don't need Peruvian real estate to create a Gulch. In fact, it's easier and better to "hide in plain sight" while transmitting encrypted ones and zeros over a distributed computer network.

Galt's plan is adopted. Midas leases an embassy from a neighboring kleptocracy to open a base of operations. Midas and Galt recruit a team of software developers, lease more property, buy a mountain fortress that overlooks a remote ex-CIA "Contra" landing strip, and hire a cadre of Russian bankers and Red Army vets for security. In three years, population of the Gulch multiplies to 50 people "hiding in plain sight" and 1,500 investors all over the world with a financial stake in encrypted banking beyond the reach of U.S. government regulators and tax collectors. The Gulch stretches from the capital diplomatic quarter to a sparsely populated province that has almost no contact with organized government. It takes four hours for cops and fire trucks to respond to emergencies, if they feel like bumping along a rutted, single-track dirt road. Groceries, building supplies and construction labor are cheap. Lush jungle, white sand beaches, supermodel beach bunnies and smiling scantily-clad native girls are bewitchingly agreeable.

*Hey, wait a minute! That Laissez Faire City thing was a scam.
People went to prison for it. Everybody lost money on it.*

Five of the signers of the Declaration of Independence were captured
by the British during the Revolutionary War. Twelve had their homes
ransacked and burned. 8,500 Americans died in British prisons and
the Continental Congress issued $400 million in worthless paper bills
— about $10 billion in today's money.

The men who suffered most in the collapse of Laissez Faire City were
its original founders and investors. Two died in prison. Three others
died before they could be captured and interrogated by authorities.

It's all very well to vilify Midas and Galt — both of whom are dead.
They gambled their lives, their fortunes, and their honor to establish
a virtual Gulch beyond the reach of government. I knew those men
personally and did everything in my power to help them. Most of the
men and women who lived and worked at Laissez Faire City gave up
professional careers to share the risk of disaster if we failed.

The chief difference between Rand's fictional Gulch and its reali-
sation at Laissez Faire City was chastity. In a utopian world of
Objectivist perfection, there is no cocaine, no scantily-clad house
maids, no hard drinking or coarse language. Rand's fictional Gulch
was isolated from the outside world — not surrounded by lawless
armed marauders and defended by gated walls, 24-hour guards, and
Rottweilers.

Surely you must be aware that Ayn Rand's personal life was far from
perfectly chaste. In 1979, at his USC office, John Hospers told me:
"She's hooked on amphetamines, totally irrational." Twenty-five
years later I wrote:

> *I believe that Ayn Rand gave us two versions of Ayn Rand... The young
> Rand was a vamp, my kind of babe. The Fountainhead had it all. Rape,
> dynamite, ruthless manipulation of weaker characters like Peter Keating,
> smashing up priceless museum pieces... Rand the seeker was an immoral
> anarchist to the very roots of her hair, top and bottom.*

The Midas Touch

A Newcomer's Humble Appraisal of The Difference Between Laissez Faire City and Galt's Gulch

Laissez Faire City Times, August 1999

After careful consideration of everything I've observed during my first two weeks in Laissez Faire City, I can say with a high degree of confidence that the difference between Galt's Gulch and this joint is — not much.

The only way to get here is by invitation like I did or by gate crashing like Dagny Taggart. If you decide to gate crash, mind the dogs. They look fierce and are fierce. I'm not at liberty to discuss some of the other security measures to keep intruders away, but I assure you that the dogs are safer. At least you can attempt to reason with a dog.

Inside Laissez Faire City, one begins to wonder why the whole world isn't organized this way. No one explained the rules to me because there aren't any, aside from the common sense prohibition of reckless contact with outsiders. Headquarters is a walled high-security laboratory designed for prodigies and Third Wave kids of all ages. It hums like a 24-hour beehive. I believe if they wanted to turn the earth physically upside down to inspect its undercarriage, they could do it. Laissez Faire City has an impressive array of brains and brawn and technical facilities, and I'll bet that I only got the 25-cent tour of half of it.

Around the corner from Headquarters, there's a four-star restaurant for LFC residents and diplomats, a hotel for LFC guests, and the sedate tree-lined campus of Rand University.

A short hop by private plane or helicopter and you arrive at my house, so to speak. I don't actually own the place. It's unlikely that anyone other than Bill Gates or Donald Trump could own such a place — a mansion on a hilltop overlooking the ocean. It requires a staff of three to keep the gardens in shape, to clean the kidney-shaped swimming pool, and run the kitchen. The land is indescribably beautiful, with every spectacular form of wildlife imaginable, including big cats. The ocean is full of marlin, sailfish, tuna, lobster, you name it. Amazingly there are no mosquitoes up here — only huge, royal blue butterflies, fuzzy gray raccoons, incredible stick insects about the size of a Parker pen, and big brown monkeys howling in the trees on the other side of my driveway.

After a night or two in a clean, comfortable room in paradise, you might be invited to visit the LFC Mountain Fortress, currently under construction. It's literally half a mountain, with enough room to rebuild Bel Air. I think they're getting close to completing the bank vaults and trading rooms. All the structural work is done, anyway — thick, reinforced concrete walls rising in tiers on the highest point for a couple hundred miles. The view is unlike anything I've ever seen before, and I've seen most of North America and Europe. There is a deeply profound sense of serenity and rightness, standing on a plinth overlooking the emerald forest and endless ocean, perceiving the curvature of the earth.

So, if we're talking about the actual differences between Laissez Faire City and Galt's Gulch, the most important discrepancy is existential. LFC is real, not fictional. It's on a mountaintop, not tucked away in some pokey valley.

There's another set of differences, largely historical in nature. We have internet clout coming out of our ears and the ability to make markets. I can only guess how much dough is being moved and traded daily in cyberspace. What I *do* know is that Laissez Faire City, despite all of its plush real estate, exists mainly as a "virtual" city that spans the globe. Two-thirds of our full-time residents live somewhere else in the world, working on screens wired to LFC and a growing population of cyber-entrepreneurs. Sorry Dagny, no diesel railroads in this version of Atlantis. You'll have to go to Philly or Boston to visit

Amtrak (if any of their trains happen to be running, instead of derailing that day). There's an old commuter line that thumps through Silicon Valley and an occasional freight train or two in Colorado, but that's about the extent of locomotion on steel in the post-industrial world. LFC uses 757 jets and Cessna turboprops for fast, friendly carriage of passengers and cargo to our neck of the woods.

Maybe that implies another structural difference between LFC and Ayn Rand's 1957 sketch of utopia. Laissez Faire City speaks several languages, including French, Russian, Polish, Danish, Dutch, and Japanese. English is spoken in two separate dialects, because the founders advertised in The Economist magazine for free-market talent. I saw a stack of letters five feet tall received in reply. LFC also recruited participants in Singapore and mainland China. This is not a pocket enclave. It's a global armada.

Most of it was the doing of one man. He doesn't want me to mention his name, so let's call him Midas. I have never before in my life met such a brilliant rascal. If anyone ever *deserved* to be rich, it's Midas. He is passionately devoted to justice and private liberty, and I have no doubt whatsoever that LFC could not have happened except for his determination to make real what Ayn Rand made fictionally hypothetical. Midas is a renaissance man in the best sense of the term. He hired me, for instance, as an artist-in-residence. My job is to stare out the window at the Pacific Ocean in the lap of luxury for a couple years and write a novel. More writers are coming — to script movies, internet cartoons, and a continuing drama (soap opera). God knows what sort of production facilities are on the drawing board, because Midas is a seasoned Hollywood producer. Guys like him tend to do things on a grand scale.

I have to say, as a personal comment, that the sculpture and "freedom art" in Laissez Faire City is wonderful to behold. Or to slap, if you're walking past the bar at Headquarters, where five solid silver, bigger than life-size busts of Hitler, Stalin, Lenin, Mao and Clinton are a constant reminder of history — above which Midas hung a giant sign: "The Butchers and Bastards of Socialism." At the front door, a stylized bronze bust of Ayn Rand greets every guest. There is never any doubt why this organization exists or whose philosophy governs it. I think it's healthy that Rand is depicted in sculpture as a beautiful woman, for she was one in spirit and she adored physical perfection, having less of it than most ladies. In Laissez Faire City, Miss Rand is a goddess at last.

Our main website mentions another hero, Napoleon Hill. It's an all or nothing challenge — to burn your bridges and leave the outside world. I had very little to burn, so it was easier in my case than others. But the actual process of closing my business, saying goodbye to the neighbors and stopping the mail with no forwarding address was a deliberately final act. No one comes to Laissez Faire City (as Thomas Jefferson said in 1776) "for light and transient causes."

Strangely, this does not make us a cult. We have folks here in every line of work — some married, some single — who have almost nothing in common with each other, except the philosophy of individualism. There are many handsome and some plain, many young and some old, a few daredevils and one or two nuts. I am happier in their company than I've ever been before in my life.

It was the last thing I expected to discover in Laissez Faire City, that I was welcome here. My work was well known, in fact better known than anywhere else on the planet. For a writer, this is heaven, to hear people casually mention something I said years ago, to have it remembered and appreciated. I'm still trying to understand it, that intelligent, courageous men like my work, that they enjoy my strange sense of humor and want more of it. This is absolutely the berries.

Our joy illustrates the moral meaning of Laissez Faire City and the principal difference between it and Galt's Gulch. LFC is real, it's fun to be here, and we're wired into the global capital markets. I'm going to be rich and famous — and you could be, too, if you join us. Please don't email me. I'm not in charge of anything except a fragment of a story idea that is vaguely coalescing into half a theme.

If your life is deeply rooted elsewhere in the world, as most lives are, don't despair. Midas and his crew are working on it. The physical community of Laissez Faire City is only a small part of our worldwide strategy.

You can participate without leaving your living room. Read this newspaper and start using PGP encryption. The City Clerk always responds favorably when people email in code. In fact, he has some software for you to test, if you ask for it in a PGP-encrypted letter that explains what you want to achieve in life. Don't be shy. I had to do the same thing in person, when the LFC recruiting sergeant knocked on my door (just joking! — he was really an admiral).

Who knows? Maybe I'll see you in one of my four deluxe guest suites, here at the embarrassingly christened "Hemingway Inn." It was Midas' idea to call it that, to remind me that he means business and expects a masterpiece from his poet in residence. Just what I always wanted, to have Ernest Hemingway staring over my left shoulder and Ayn Rand sitting on my head, while I work on a novel. This is indubitably the bottom line at Laissez Faire City.

We be champions, bubba.

A Writer's Temple

G21 Magazine, Feb. 2000

It didn't take long. Folks are upset because fate handed me a mansion on the Pacific, no job, no bills, no household chores (cocktail parties and fan mail optional). Temporarily rich, I'm learning how to push an intercom button and order breakfast when I feel like it in the morning. Queenie bought a young chestnut stallion, hand picked by the gardener's brother. A fine horse indeed according to its trainer and heartily concurred by our housekeeper, the relief housekeeper, the downstairs maid, and a leatherfaced blacksmith.

But if I'm going to be envied for anything, I'd rather be scolded for having a writer's temple. If you don't have one, be assured it is the goal of all human industry — farms, oil wells, semi-conductor factories, etc. Paradoxically, I did very little to achieve possession of a writer's temple. You can set one up for about 30 cents, and it's completely portable. I've carried this particular temple around the planet with me for the better part of two decades. It fits with any decor (although a bare room is best). Here are the specs:

- desk

- chair

- computer

- printer

- lamp

- bed

So what makes it a temple? — Chrissie Hynde tonight, Led Zeppelin tomorrow, and a minimum of contact with the outside world, including my wife. We get together between bouts of writing that run for a day or two, before I overheat and need hospitalization. My recurring mental exhaustion doesn't play well in Queenie's boudoir, so I limit my time in the temple to six or seven hours a day, and I learned to take a lot of leisurely breaks. Having houseguests has been helpful (provided they leave after a few days). But temple life doesn't end simply because I take time off. Indeed, time away must end in my return. I always return to writing, whether I want to or not.

That's why my temple is a masterpiece of efficiency. Left to right on the desk top are: carton of Marlboro, telephone, intercom, legal pad, stack of CDs, ashtray, small pile of notes, coffee cup, mouse pad, and a big empty area to park stuff in transit. People ask me to read things. They sit in the Transit Area for a month or two and ultimately get shoved in a drawer.

In the event that I have to relocate my writing temple, the desk drawers are emptied, and I say a little ceremonial "Hmm" over a black plastic trash bag, to honor the forgotten. These paper orphans are omelet parts, in the sense that they sacrifice their thin, rectangular lives, so that my temple is not defiled by accounting statements, story outlines, or vital correspondence.

I follow an exacting rule, adapted from the One Minute Manager: handle everything only once, and put all of it immediately in a thick, neat pile that deters further involvement.

I cannot write any other way. The temple computer is always on, and my screen has no games, no cutesy icons, no ICQ flower. Bookmarks are few: just G21 and two other publication venues, and an archive of my defunct website. This last item shows how hard it is to achieve defunctnitude on the web. I canceled my London mirror account more than a year ago and repeatedly begged them by email to delete the subdomain. All I achieved was to lock myself out of their firewall and the site is still live, proving that this author does not comprehend the Internet.

It's highly debatable that I understand anything at all, since story outlines are useless to me. I pen them in good faith. But however daring and clever, an outline only controls one character, usually less than a week or two — which is enough to belt out the first chapter. From there, the story takes off on its own, surprising me with situations and personalities over which I have no direct control. The temple has its own agenda, it's own mad logic of dramatic necessity. All I do is show up to write about it.

Therefore, a temple. Sometimes it's frightening and lonely and empty. I feel like shit and walk away. The story follows me to the kitchen, to the driveway, to a sunset or the night sky. I whistle for the dogs and pretend that I'm a normal person — that, no matter what, I'm just as fit as the next fellow to have a private life, I can eat a meal or chat with houseguests.

Writers tell themselves lies like that, to avoid the truth of the temple. Quality doesn't matter much, nor hope.

The essence of the issue is a blank page and the willingness to go naked in public. As far as I know, Victor Hugo already beat me hands down. What remains is a precious window of courage, to let it happen and let it be.

'The Good Walk Alone' was serialized 16 consecutive weeks in Laissez Faire City Times, 1999-2000 (above the fold)

Janet DiMarco is a reality-oriented heroine for all seasons and willing to take whatever comes next. Winning or losing is not her criteria for purposeful destiny. No matter who wins, DiMarco lays her life on the line for law and order. Can you blame her? Who else could she trust to do the right thing, the difficult thing, her sworn duty as a cop.

Liberty

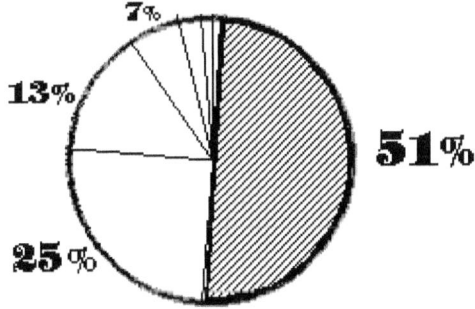

Competence

Broadly speaking, the free exercise of liberty is a limitless horizon, if you have the courage and capacity to take action, accept the risk and suffer accordingly. There is no such thing as a free ride.

A newborn baby is extremely vulnerable, utterly powerless for a few seconds until it begins to breathe unaided. I have a vivid recollection of my daughter's birth 12 years ago. She did not volunteer to be born and had no capacity to select her parents or the century in which she was thrust and thereby challenged to discover and exercise liberty.

Tragic births are far worse. Some children have no meaningful chance in life, no power to overcome their fate as perpetual victims of their physical and mental limitations, bad parenting, poverty, destructive social influences, religion, conscription and tribal war. Freedom is a relatively recent and privileged estate among the billions of children born throughout history. Objectivist families are a small minority. We operate in a broadly hostile world with very few allies.

Some argue that liberty is destined to triumph as a political ideal. At an ISIL conference sponsored by Laissez Faire City, Milton Friedman suggested that Fabianism (municipal gas, water and sewer socialism) was so old and weary as an ideology that it would inevitably yield to new improved principles of libertarianism. Francis Fukuyama made a similar claim in The End of History, citing the fall of communism.

I could demolish both of those silly fallacies in five minutes. But it's more important to stay on topic. Liberty is not a social philosophy or broadly implemented political system. In the freest and least coercive state, some children will be born healthy and some not. Some parents are fit to raise healthy children; others are less able to resist the maw of misplaced expectations, hardships, and social pressures.

It is not a matter of wealth, but rather the hard facts of reality that determine whether a parent is fit to raise children. Suppose you are standing on a freeway overpass, with traffic racing below at highway speed. You attempt to leap from the overpass onto a semi's trailer as it shoots out ten feet below, a reasonably easy distance to jump down. But the moment you leap for it, your 18-wheeler is long gone, and if you time the right moment to jump so that you land on the roof of its trailer, it would be certain death, like smashing into a wall at 70 mph. Parenting is not a Hollywood movie stunt with trick photography.

Rich or poor, the decision to become a parent is an extreme example of exercising one's liberty with profound consequences. No man or woman is fully competent to predict the outcome. Very often, the act of copulation and impregnation is a matter of transcendent passion.

Objectivists know what they're doing and why. Pregnancy is not an unwanted surprise. Mom and Dad know that it means decades of personal sacrifice and tough decisions from day to day in answer to unpredictable, unexpected, myriad questions of what might be best for the kid in novel or adverse situations. No one does this perfectly. There are tears to shed and terrible transits of regret and despair.

All children suffer injuries. It's a necessary step in learning to exercise their liberty. No child can be (or ought to be) supervised every split-second of every day. They slip and fall. They explore storm drains, catch snakes, get stung by bees and thrown off horses, collect bruises and head lice and intestinal viruses. They have to be shown kitchen equipment, sharp knives, boiling water, ovens, and hot pad holders.

Their dreams and ambitions matter. Shortly before her 12th birthday, my daughter became sad, silent, deeply troubled and withdrawn. I let it go for a day or two. Privacy is the existential fountainhead of growth. But her silence persisted longer than I thought was healthy, so I knocked on her bedroom door and sat down. She didn't want to talk about it. I promised not to tell Mom. I promised not to laugh or think she was crazy. Eventually she unwound enough to tell me. She wanted to travel in outer space to other star systems.

I told her that it might be possible during her lifetime. Not during my lifetime, but perhaps in hers. I explained that to become an astronaut, she would first have to learn how to fly an airplane. Thinking of that moment again, just now, I burst into tears. They are streaming down my cheeks as I write. Fatherhood is an emotional business.

Her pilot's flight bag is in the living room, a heavy black vinyl thing on wheels with zipper pockets stuffed full of manuals and checklists and maps and flight calculators; no different than the flight bag you'd see a commercial pilot wheel along into the cockpit of his 747.

She completed aviation ground school in four months, the youngest candidate at age 12, and now has 5 hours logged as Pilot Flying with her instructor as a co-pilot. She learned to do the complete pre-flight engine, fuel, and control surface checks. She did her own taxiing and takeoffs and landings, sitting on a pillow so she could see over the instrument panel. I watched her take off in a strong crosswind. My heart was in my throat as her plane wobbled aloft.

When she was 10 years old, I watched her trot and canter and jump a huge stallion over four-foot fences, keeping his head high, whipping him to keep pace and leap again. We don't grow children by keeping them safe.

Some time in the past year, she began to menstruate — a matter that she and Mom had prepared for and which I'm not permitted to have any explicit knowledge of. Not quite 13, she has become a woman.

A couple nights ago, I took a break from writing and laid down to rest for a few minutes. Suddenly, I burst out laughing. My daughter has no idea of what the next few years will be like, with boys tripping over themselves to strike up conversations, ask questions, brag about their prowess, offer to carry her bag of school books. The problem of growing up is a never ending practical joke on all concerned.

No one is adequately prepared for the challenge of life and liberty.

THE *51%*

SOLUTION

Written and circulated privately in 1994
published in booklet form by Cthonia Press 1997
republished by Laissez Faire City Times 1999

Let's start by defining our terms. A value is something you want to gain or keep. A lot of people think that life is a fundamental value, to be preserved at all costs. "Family values" are a bundle of warm fuzzies: taking the kids to a park, teaching them to be nice people, helping each other through life's difficulties. Values are conditions we deem to be good. They are outcomes that require effort to achieve and maintain, something worth fighting for.

Virtue is a purposeful action required to obtain or defend a value. The American Founding Fathers declared that freedom was a fundamental right; they pledged their lives, their fortunes, and their sacred honor to the battle for American independence. If you are married to someone you love, the virtues of fidelity and honesty are actions that preserve an intimate partnership. If you are a banker, fidelity and honesty must be practiced to keep your job.

Basic definitions concluded, we come to the controversial topic of standards. The purpose of a standard is to enable us to measure things — like the distance between London and San Francisco (5358 miles, flying a Great Circle route, about 10 hours).

Let's say, for instance, you decide that being rich is your No. 1 priority. If wealth is your basic standard of value, you'll measure everything in life according to its financial consequences. Telling someone the truth suddenly becomes a lot less important. Deciding who to marry is a question of which bachelor or heiress has the biggest fortune or the greatest potential of earning one. If the Ten Commandments are your standard of value and virtue, everything in life is measured according to whether it was mentioned by Moses. Islamic revolutionaries select actions and targets according to the obligation of jihad. Zen masters organize their day around tea ceremonies and try to rid themselves of distracting passions. Catholic nuns and monks concentrate their efforts on transcendant communion with God, or they serve the needy, depending on which particular saint inspired their vows.

Moral standards, therefore, tend to organize values and virtues into a hierarchical scheme. Fertile young women of child-bearing age are usually interested in finding a suitable husband, a good doctor, a comfortable home, good schools, safe neighborhoods, physical fitness, child psychology, nutrition, the prevention of infectious disease and a thousand other details pertaining to offspring, marriage, and family life. The central organizing principle or standard of value in this case is the welfare of her children. To a military commander, top priority is the welfare of his troops, expressed in dozens of specific concerns: training, equipment, supplies, logistics, morale, command structure, communications, tactical use of diversion and surprise, how to retreat, etc. Pilots focus on flying the airplane and landing in one piece.

Myth, Morality and Moderation

Most people conduct themselves like pilots. They navigate their lives away from danger and toward successful outcomes, measuring success in terms of comfort, pleasure, acceptance by their peers, and a sense of mastery or achievement. The whole point of living is to get good at it, to see yourself as a competent individual, whose personal values were realized by virtuous pursuits and dutiful labor.

Historically, this common sense morality did not prevent people from joining the Nazis or the Communist Party, both of which offered comfort, pleasure, and social approval to millions of citizens who aspired to be "good Germans" and "pioneers of Socialism". The folks who followed Jim Jones to Guyana, and David Koresh to Waco, thought they were part of a success oriented, life sustaining enterprise. No one joined the parade thinking it would lead them to death and disgrace, that their children would be murdered, that their capacity to love would be recklessly extinguished by a charismatic fool.

It is no excuse that the victims of fascism or fanatic religious cults were "brainwashed." Whoever you are, American citizen or stateless refugee, innocent child or college graduate, your brain has been washed by a thousand years of received wisdom, an ocean of culture. The young always follow their parents. We follow each other, because our survival is tied to social integration. Manufacturers make products that people really want. Politicians advocate policies that flatter and appease their constituents. In America the penalty for expressing an unpopular opinion is political defeat, poverty and ridicule. In China the penalty is prison "re-education" until you recant and beg for mercy. The difference is only in degree of severity.

The overwhelming need to get along with one's neighbors, to accommodate and reiterate the dominant moral standard of one's culture, is a shared experience communicated from one generation to the next in the form of symbols and myths. The Stars and Stripes are symbolic of the moral standard implied in the Declaration of Independence — that all men are endowed by their Creator with certain inalienable rights.

The mythic exploits of Abraham Lincoln, Martin Luther King, and John F. Kennedy are vital components of every grade school curriculum. I think of them particularly in connection with the 1960s pop song "Abraham, Martin and John" – a tearful tribute to three slain moral crusaders who heroically sacrificed their lives for the betterment of humanity. In mythological terms, this is identical to the crucifixion of Jesus, who sacrificed himself for the redemption of ignorant sinners and inspired David Koresh to end his life in a blaze of glory.

Historical accuracy is not central to (or typical of) mythological moral standards. Neither is rationality. They exist because technical statements of good and evil are too sublime and intellectually challenging for ordinary people to comprehend. It is much easier to remember the mythical story of Jesus and obey His commandment to love one another – without asking why or demanding proof that Jesus was quoted accurately by biblical witnesses.

Nor is it likely that an average person will attempt to govern his life 100% in conformity to a mythological standard. Mythical heroes are intended to open one's eyes, not to close them happily ever after.

The job of living is infinitely complex. No myth, no received wisdom can exempt you from the direct, immediate task of sizing up your situation and making the best decision you can, often in stressful circumstances. Slogans and symbols do not tell you how to conduct your life in detail, nor would you want to obey unquestioningly someone else's creed.

Ayn Rand said, "The moral is the chosen, not the forced." If you have no choice, you have no moral responsibility or personal participation in the outcome.

Too timid to be a hero, too skeptical to blindly follow their neighbors, most people find themselves in agreement with Aristotle, who said that moral virtue consists of practicing moderation. A little wealth, a little compromise, a little courage, a little gratitude – constantly seeking the middle of the road leads to longevity and happiness. Against this, Western philosophy offered three important criticisms: that moderation is a prevarication (Ayn Rand), that personal happiness is an immoral standard of value (Immanuel Kant), and that human beings are innately evil (Thomas Hobbes).

Small wonder that ordinary people feel uncertain about the source and meaning of moral values. Huddled together in spiritual darkness, we find ourselves drawn to family values and silently pray that no one in the family forces us to examine or explain the difference between good and evil. Confronted with a moral dilemma, our first impulse is to forgive and judge not, lest we be judged, too.

We practice the ethics of moral mice, fearful of being seen in the light of day, nibbling on life's crumbs, terrified that our inexperienced offspring will wander too far from the nest and encounter the cat of philosophy.

Orders of Magnitude

It is not my purpose to indict anyone, nor to urge upon you a tough new moral standard. Rather, I should like to introduce a simple method for measuring value and virtue, based on the fundamental concept of measurement itself. To explain my theory, it is necessary to define two basic elements of logic: unit and predicate. It's a little boring, but stay with me for a couple of pages and then decide if it makes sense.

"Unit" is the first principle of arithmetic.[1]

In order to count 1, 2, 3, you must begin with the notion of "one", a uniform and constant unit of measurement. When we say that the flying distance between London and San Francisco is 5358 miles, approximately 10 hours by nonstop commercial aircraft, we are saying that units of measurement (miles, hours) are constant and interchangeable. Mile #1 is exactly the same length as Mile #2 and every other mile in the journey. Hour 1 is exactly the same duration as Hour 2, both in the air and on the ground. Miles and hours can be used to measure and compare all journeys, all methods of transportation, etc.

In discussing my theory of value, we will need to accept as axiomatic that two is twice as big as one. For the purpose of this essay, the relationship is deemed an order of magnitude.[2]

"Predicate" is the first principle of language and classical logic. It is also the central bone of contention in Western philosophy, theology, and politics.

Say, for instance, that you are at a birthday party with a number of others. You decide to count the number attending the party: 1, 2, 3, 4, 5, 6, 7, 8. But eight units of what? – of men and women, boys and girls. You could have also said that there were eight "people" at the party, but children aren't quite the same as adults, and therefore we habitually count them as members of a different class. Likewise, it is customary and useful to distinguish between male people and female people, referring to them respectively as "men" and "women" on the doors of segregated rest rooms. Not so many years ago, it was customary to distinguish between caucasians and negroes, referring to them respectively as Whites and Colored on the doors of segregated rest rooms.

Whether we prefer to call someone a "woman", a "female", a "negro", an "American", or a "person" is not the point. Rather, the point is that predicates are inescapable, when you count persons, things, or values.

To predicate something (P) of something else (Q) is to identify an attribute or quality that makes unit Q a member of class P:

> Wolf is a person.
> Socrates is musical.
> All deer are ruminants.
> Some birds cannot fly.

In discussing my theory of value, we will need to accept as axiomatic that a class subsumes and refers to all of the units or members of that class, and that it is impossible for a predicate to be both true and false at the same time. This impossibility is known as a contradiction.

More or Less Value?

Russian-born writer Ayn Rand, following Aristotle, advanced the two axioms of measurement already discussed, plus a third notion: that values are ordinate numbers.

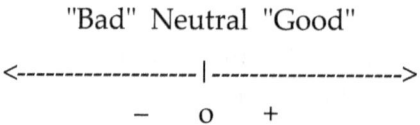

Values are positive, making life worth living, or advancing our dignity as human beings. Whatever we deem to be good is neither indifferent nor bad. Ayn Rand concluded that reason was the ultimate good, that rationality was the ultimate virtue, and that human life was the proper standard of value. Personally, I'm not so sure.

As an artist, I've never cared a heck of a lot about my life. I smoke cigarettes, take enormous financial risks, and don't value myself very highly at all. To me, the ultimate good is artistic achievement. Living is only a means.

I think I'm in good company (no pun intended). The American Revolutionary patriots cared more for liberty than personal survival. They were willing to risk everything, including their families, to free themselves from a tyrant. Heroism is not just a myth; people really do lay down their lives for values like freedom and justice.

Therefore I've discarded half of Ayn Rand's theory of value. Instead of a two-directional ordinate scale, mine goes from zero to infinity.

No Value . . . . . "Good"

|---|---|---|---|---|---|---|---|---|---|---|--->

0 1 2 3 4 5 6 7 8 9 10 +

Observe that my scale of value is divided into units of value. I think values can be expressed numerically, and that the correct way to measure value is in orders of magnitude. If my ultimate personal "good" is artistic achievement and I arbitrarily give it the numerical value of 10, then whatever class of value is next in my personal hierarchy of "goodness" (survival, for instance) only deserves a 5, because 5 is an order of magnitude smaller than 10. It keeps things in their proper perspective: **X is my highest value and Y is the next most important value, but only half as important as X.**

This way, there is never any confusion about a standard of value, because the unit-value of my ultimate No. 1 personal priority out-numbers everything else put together.

WOLF'S PERSONAL VALUES

Magnitude	Value Class	Unit Value
No. 1	Artistic achievement	= 10.0
...all the others summed together		= 9.84375
No. 2	Survival/comfort	= 5
No. 3	Social approval	= 2.5
No. 4	Helping others	= 1.25
No. 5	Political power	= 0.625
No. 6	Place in history	= 0.3125
No. 7	Talent to amuse	= 0.15625

I hope and trust that this makes some sense to you, at least on the intuitive level. If values are not expressed as orders of magnitude, they tend to contradict each other and pretty quickly you lose sight of your standard of value (your ultimate No. 1 priority). In my own life, for example, I occasionally catapult priority No. 7 to the top of my list and try to tell jokes. Friends and family often point out that this is not a particularly good idea, since I'm rarely funny, and it's an occasion to remember that Humor is a relatively small magnitude in the universe of my values.

We are only at the beginning, the theoretical starting point of how to measure value and virtue. But I think you can see the direction I'm taking: an ultimate value must have real value, meaning and weight, sufficient to inspire and outweigh all of your subordinate wishes and hopes. Whatever is first in your life deserves a majority of your loyalty, effort, conviction, and courage. We expect mothers to put the welfare of her children ahead of her own. We require our military commanders to put the welfare of his troops ahead of any personal ambition, and certainly not to sacrifice them uselessly or recklessly for abstract glory. We expect pilots to fly the damn airplane and get us down safely, with no spiritual conflict of interest at 36,000 feet over Greenland.

The 51% Solution

By nature, I'm a conservative businessman. I don't like 50/50 partnerships, because they always result in a deadlock over some trivial decision. It's much better to have a majority interest, even if it's only 51%. That way you can't be outvoted by minority shareholders.

I trust you have already guessed what this has to do with moral values: the No. 1 value must command a majority of your loyalty and virtue, or else all the disgruntled lesser values could vote as a bloc and kick your No. 1 value-standard out of the executive suite.

Moreover, to be the boss implies the power to hire and fire subordinates. If No. 7 is disruptive, working against overall corporate policy, and embarrassing everybody else on the team, he ought to be fired. I've never had the heart to absolutely banish my love of comedy but it was demoted several times, from No. 3 to No. 7, and if Humor doesn't serve its immediate superior, a Place In History, then watch out, it'll end up peeling potatoes, right next to value No. 68, Good Housekeeping.

The task of putting your spiritual house in order is largely a mathematical process. Make something your majority interest, the boss, the Prime Directive. Give it 51% of your time and attention – i.e., the virtue of acting in accordance with your ultimate purpose.

Once you have chosen that first order of value, you still have 49% left to devote to something else, usually several something elses.

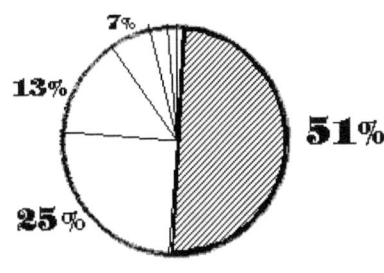

As a practical matter, the Top Five are really all you need to consider, since they account for 97% of your values, even if you meticulously calculate an infinity of smaller magnitudes. For example, I seldom think about winning a Place In History (personal value No. 6). It's way down my list of priorities and tends to get pushed aside.

The Top Five are a lot, both numerically and spiritually. Rare indeed is the happy saint whose 51% is never distracted or tempted by a second priority – like food or rest, for instance. His 51% is to love God with his whole heart and his whole mind, hunger or fatigue be damned. As an artist, I am intimately familiar with inner conflicts, because survival keeps howling at the door of my ivory tower: rent, food, gasoline, postage, you name it. Value No. 3, Approval tears my guts out every time I submit a work of art. Who among us does not want to be accepted, included, appreciated and praised by others?

The specific details are unimportant, but I've had six screenplays, fifty essays, two books, and a television series tossed in the trashcan by Society. If social approval was my 51% – my ultimate standard of value – I'd be learning how to produce something more popular.

But value No. 3 (13%) is nothing compared to No. 2 (25%) in terms of inner turmoil. The second banana is always challenging No. 1 (51%), always doubting his moral leadership and criticizing the outcome. Like jealous siblings, your first and second notions of "goodness" compete for moral supremacy – i.e., to be recognized as Prime Directive, governing all else in your spiritual life.

Class Warfare

Perhaps you'll recall that my No. 2 was a hyphenated notion of goodness: Survival/Comfort. I used those words because I thought it would be easier for you to understand, rather than the technical term Marginal Utility, which is pleasure greater than pain, in an economic universe wherein maximum pleasure results from uniform want-satisfaction.

Whether we call it Survival/Comfort or marginal utility or something else is unimportant. What I'd like you to consider is the generality of this concept. It embraces an economic theory, a standard of value, and a thousand details of "goodness" and "virtue". This is the power and meaning of a conceptual predicate: a class of value-units that belong together and derive scope because they have an implicitly shared purpose.

For instance, being Happily Married is subsumed and included. So is paying the rent on time, eating fresh food, buying a new pair of shoes, and doing part-time jobs that make use of my skills (sound system engineering, video production) instead of working for minimum wage as an unskilled laborer. Marginal utility results in want-satisfaction on the carnal plane of life: pleasure greater than pain. It is governed by the principle of diminishing returns, such as the declining enjoyment of successive bites of food.

> *The amount of one and the same enjoyment diminishes continuously as we proceed with that enjoyment without interruption, until satiety is reached.*
> (Hermann Heinrich Gossen)

Every aspect of Survival/Comfort involves some sort of trade-off between pleasure and pain. Marginal utility is the common sense strategy of maximizing pleasure. To be happily married, I must love and honor my wife, remain faithful and honest, no matter how uncomfortable it makes me, from time to time, when I have to admit an embarrassing truth, and work at making the relationship suc-cessful. It's worth the effort because I have a particularly wonderful partner: she knows and understands that my 51% is devoted to something other than being happily married or paying the rent. Her love, her moral support, the beauty of her soul and her intimate trust easily outweigh the pain I experience shopping, cooking dinner, hearing idiotic soap operas on our TV set, and knowing that someday we will be parted by illness and death. This is marginal utility in a nutshell. It is better to cherish my wife and someday lose her, than to have never loved at all.

I hope you will accept my word for it, that being married to Queenie is terribly dear to my heart[3] and that I receive enormous physical and spiritual pleasure from being married to her. Perhaps you will also take my word for it, that it cuts me to the quick, whenever I have to say "We can't afford to buy fresh food today" or "I bounced three checks, and the overdraft charges are going to wipe out everything I earned last week". The value of Survival/Comfort always finds a willing ally in Social Approval, ruthlessly attacking my soul for wasting 51% of my effort on something utterly devoid of utility – something so painful, with no commensurate return on investment, that no sensible person would want it: the unprofitable pursuit of Artistic Achievement.

Even now, in this moment, I am painfully aware of the cost. It is highly unlikely that this essay will ever return a penny to me. The rent and utilities are past due, but I postponed making money or looking for work, in order to write a sermon about morality! I haven't spent two minutes with Queenie in a week, except for a peck on the cheek, because my whole concentration was devoted to a non-profit lecture on a subject that no one will likely publish. If published, it will neither pay the rent nor rehabilitate my reputation in Hollywood. If anything, publication of this essay will push me farther away from career opportunities as a filmmaker, and make it harder to write marketable potboilers.

It is imperative at this juncture to erase from your mind everything I've said about Queenie, Hollywood, survival, and Wolf's internal value-conflicts. Please consider instead what is meant by an abstract predicate of value.

The term "artistic achievement" does not refer to one specific instance of achievement, nor to a precise outcome that can be gained by following a formula for success. The value of an artist's career is determined by an enormously complex context, including his native talents, his cultural environment, the history of art, and a long chain of events (study, experimentation, spiritual development) that may or may not culminate in a body of works. Acceptance of those works by others is irrelevant to the artist, because he is primarily concerned with his own subjective evaluation of the outcome as a lifelong process of inner refinement. It is an evolving, abstract statement of value that cannot be reduced to a laundry list of want-satisfactions. Indeed, the outcome cannot be described in advance. Every artist embarks upon the quest for achievement with the knowledge that he will probably fail. Painters are in competition with Vermeer and Monet. Writers must exceed the benchmarks of excellence set by Victor Hugo and Simone de Beauvoir. Anything less is failure – and the structure of achievement is undefined. One can only paint or write with his whole heart, struggling to reach something beautiful, original and previously nonexistent.

I do not claim any such achievement. Nor the courage to continue. All I want you to consider and understand is that values are not laundry lists. It is nonsense to define one's priorities as 51% new car, 25% marry Elmo, 13% have a child, 7% lose weight, and 4% save for a rainy day.

Values are abstractions: to love and obey God (Moses), to establish justice (Madison), to respect others (Kant), to win by any means necessary (Machiavelli). I won't urge you to pick any of these as your standard of value. But consciously or unconsciously, every one of us is seeking an abstract goal in life. Yours may be petty or profound, the result of fear or fortitude, knowledge or guesswork. And no one is free to suddenly choose or discard a standard of value, like ready-to-wear clothing, because moral life is an organic evolution that began on the day you were born.

Acorns and Oak Trees

To learn anything about morality, we have to accept the idea that reality is real: that acorns grow into oak trees, and never become halibuts or eagles. Growth does not occur backwards, with mature trees shrinking into seeds and leaping from the ground back into parental buds. Photosynthesis does not emit light back to the Sun, and time cannot be reversed, despite a half-century of science fiction. Your moral life is real: it grows from innocent childhood to maturity.

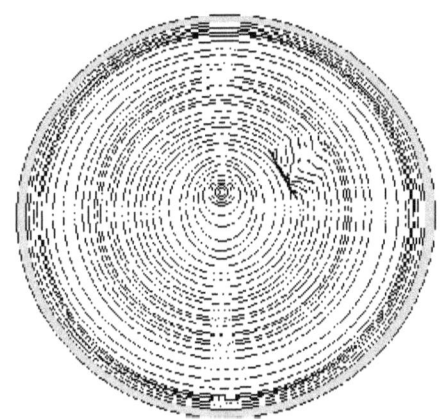

I have reproduced this illustration of a tree trunk, felled at age 47, to discuss the history of its life, recorded in the size and shape of its annual growth rings. At five years old the slender tree, growing straight, was knocked sideways by the fall of a neighbor. It reacted by growing twice as strongly on the lower side in an attempt to correct its slant. When the tree was 14 years old a ground-fire swept through the forest. The bark and cambium on the windward side were destroyed. In subsequent years they grew over the wound by degrees. It took six years to close it completely.

Other trees growing around gradually deprived the tree of light and robbed it of moisture. When it was 27 years old, "thinning" of the woods brought it suddenly into the open. There was a great leap in growth rate, still visible in the rings. Six years of rapid growth followed. Then came a drought; its effects are visible for six rings.

If somebody sawed your soul in half, they'd be able to see a permanent record like the annual growth rings of a tree. As slender young spirits, we recover from all but the most fatal assaults. In adolescence, the wounds of firey passion take years to heal by degrees. Our socialization with others deprives us of moral independence and spiritual sustenance. In adulthood, some people "thin" themselves from the dense forest of conformity: rapid moral growth follows. And then comes a drought, because they are no longer part of the anonymous consensus. Standing alone, their spiritual growth depends entirely on whatever goodness and mercy they can catch by themselves.

 Look again at the illustration of the tree. The pointed scar in the upper right quadrant was caused by an injury, and for many years the tree struggled to heal itself by focussing its energies on that wound. People do exactly the same thing. Told by Catholic nuns that her soul was black, my wife struggled for years to develop the independent moral conviction that the Church was wrong, that it was impossible for a child's soul to be black at birth. Her spiritual wound was healed slowly, a little bit at a time, as she studied and lived and grew more confident in the knowledge that her own mind was competent to examine and challenge the centuries-old dogma of Original Sin. For all those years, during which Queenie was engaged in healing the spiritual wound she suffered as a child, her 51% was deeply devoted to rebuilding her sense of moral competence.

The exigencies of life challenge each person with an unique set of moral crises, a cultural time and place to be reckoned with and overcome. The battle for control of your soul does not end with college education, or wealthy parents, or commercial success. If anything, these "advantages" make it increasingly harder to resist the received wisdom of philosophers, parents, role models, customers and cheering crowds. If you take nothing else from this essay, think again of your progress in life and ask yourself: How much of it was mine by choice? Joseph Campbell tells the following story in The Power of Myth[4]:

> Before I was married, I used to eat out in the restaurants of town for my lunch and dinners. Thursday night was the maid's night off in Bronxville, so that many of the families were out in restaurants.

One fine evening I was in my favorite restaurant there, and at the next table there was a father, a mother, and a scrawny boy about twelve years old. The father said to the boy, "Drink your tomato juice." And the boy said, "I don't want to."

Then the father, with a louder voice, said, "Drink your tomato juice." And the mother said, "Don't make him do what he doesn't want to do."

The father looked at her and said, "He can't go through life doing what he wants to do. If he does only what he wants to do, he'll be dead. Look at me. I've never done a thing I wanted to in all my life."

And I thought, "My God, there's Babbitt incarnate!"

That's a man who never followed his bliss. You may have success in life, but then just think of it – what kind of life was it? What good was it? – you've never done the thing you wanted to do in all your life. I always tell my students, go where your body and soul want to go. When you have the feeling, then stay with it, and don't let anyone throw you off.

Going where your body and soul want to go is called egoism, or self-interest, or just plain selfishness. It is culturally frowned upon as moral wrong-doing, and many Western philosophers have labored to demonstrate that doing what you want to do is unethical.

The Church said as much to Galileo, and England sent her redcoats by the thousands to quash the American Declaration of Independence. Without urging you to take one side or another, I suggest you read Thomas Jefferson's version of inalienable human rights.

Risk and Reward

It is not my purpose to agitate for a universal moral standard that applies to everyone. Frankly, I have enough trouble figuring out what to do with the unique problems of my own life, and I am convinced that very little can be gleaned from my personal struggle. I am a mystery to myself most of the time. All I know is that my 51%, for better or worse, is devoted to a passion that few people care about.

Most people are concerned with earning a living and caring for their children, which are honorable virtues in my opinion. While waiting to speak to a client yesterday, I had to wait in the restaurant area. A mother and father, age 30-something, sat down at a pair of tables nearby with their four children, all bright-faced boys, ages 4, 6, 7 and 9. It was obvious to me in an instant of observation that Mom and Dad devoted every waking minute of their lives to the task of rearing those children.

If you have children, God bless you and keep you from losing whatever happiness might be yours and theirs. If you do not yet have children – that is: if your life is still yours to spend in some meaningful sense, I have one more topic to discuss: the equation of risk and reward.

As the word "equation" implies, risk = reward, but it is important to remember that equivalent terms are identical. Taking a risk is the reward. There is no other reward, except departing from the safety of your known values and undertaking an adventure with uncertain consequences. In fact, most people who put themselves at risk end up losing something in the bargain. It is a maxim in Nevada, never to gamble unless you are prepared to lose.

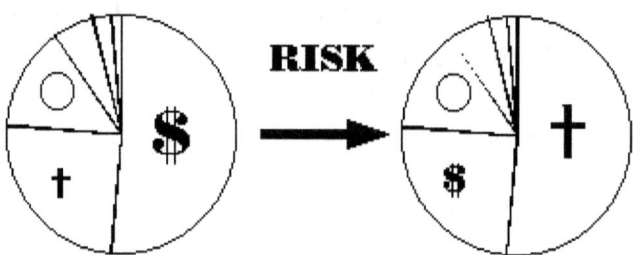

For simplicity in the accompanying chart, I used the $ symbol to represent Survival/Comfort and the cross to represent religious ideals. The circle represents leisure time. At left, Mr. X values money first, God second, and leisure third. He is considering whether to love God more than utilitarian Survival/Comfort. The risk is substantial, because he will have to completely rearrange his life, if he is to honestly pursue the new Prime Directive of religious values.

Worse: there is no guarantee that he will succeed in this new venture, or that his understanding of God's will is even partly correct. He cannot consult the Almighty in advance, nor could he comprehend the Supreme Being's purpose if God spoke to him.

I leave you with hope, each of you in every walk of life, that your 51% brings you comfort in your later years, that the god of your moral universe is one you will learn to understand through the hardship of seeking it, and that your subsidiary values and wishes don't mutiny too often. There is a story I remember whenever the burden of life seems too great, and my values are warring among themselves, each one claiming to be less cowardly.

Mohammed was visiting the encampment of a great army, escorted by a cadre of hardened generals. They passed by one of the many injured, who involuntarily groaned with pain, because he had been horribly wounded. "Silence!" the generals ordered, "You must not cry in the presence of the Holy Prophet!"

But Mohammed raised both of his hands, as a sign to the generals to refrain from reprimanding the wounded man, and said to them, in forgiveness and in peace: "Let him groan, for groaning also is one of the names of God."

Mohammed's compassion seems feeble to me, for it cured no one of their suffering, and it did not abolish the cause of painful experience. Our moral life is one story told many times – of experiments gone wrong, of hopes dashed, and life's short span never attaining the perfection we believed would be ours.

But I offer feeble compassion because I feel it firstly for myself, and I urge you to feel something similar, especially when you screw up in the values department. It requires courage to admit that your 51% is (or was) misguided. Having said you were wrong about something is the first step toward making an improvement, for which you should be praised, not punished.

I have been wrong many, many times. Each time, I forgave myself after a lot of weepy, painful groaning. These emotional experiences are purposeful and necessary, however much we hate them.

NOTES:

1. adapted from Rand, Introduction to Objectivist Epistemology. The simplified restatement of her theory, presented above, is my view of a technically complex and important question.

2. In astronomy, an "order of magnitude" is 10 times greater.

3. This essay was written 20 years ago. I am married someone else now. Values and relationships are not written in stone. Artistic achievement is no longer my #1 value. Children are always first, never second in the life of a loving parent.

4. Joseph Campbell, The Power of Myth, with Bill Moyers (New York: Doubleday 1988). "Babbitt" refers to the main character in a Sinclair Lewis novel of that name. The theme of self-abnegation and conformity appears in the literature of every country in the world.

The Forbidden Self

adapted from a letter to my adult son, Robert

I will make an effort to explain the central question that we face as individuals, nations, and pawns of history. In the busy chaos of seven billion lives — some rich, many poor — it seems silly to assert a common thread, much less a universal human condition. But it's true. All of humanity are equally threatened by one shared dilemma and one common enemy.

It is often said that "power corrupts." On its face, this seems undeniable. In fact, I wrote a pretty wonderful script in 1981 that gushed Lord Acton's epigram with widescreen enthusiasm — so, I was no less a parrot of common sense in my youth. Faced with cruelty in every walk of life, trusting no one, it is easy and natural to conclude that power is the root of all evil. I propose to change your mind about conventional wisdom. Standby for a shock. Power is the root of human goodness.

I will stipulate that power can be abused, misused, forsaken, wasted, etc. This does not change the fundamental issue. Some are powerful and others are not. At the base of all human power is **intelligence**, the fountainhead of weapons and lifesaving drugs, the permanent and exclusive source of wealth. Before human power can be wrongly applied, somebody has to be bright enough to discover and transform raw potential, unleashing its power. Before downstream consequences allegedly mock his intention, some courageous pioneer has to plan and build a furnace, roll the gun barrels and test-fly a prototype. These things do not pop into existence without invention. Nor are they an anonymous, collective product that we all somehow helped to make possible. Reason is not a play group. Every historic achievement in business, industry, medicine, aviation, finance, agricultural science and mining was the work of a *few* who disobeyed and enlightened the *many*.

You can argue that pollution is a hateful scourge, that war and violence are evil consequences of man's genius. But the facts do not support hysterical fantasies of doom. In reality, mankind are more peaceful, healthier, and less frightened today than at any previous time in human history. Why? — because science triumphed over superstition. The few taught the many how to farm, how to make steel, how to build bridges and sail ships, how to negotiate instead of feuding, how to frustrate tyranny and extend the rule of law, how to pool private savings and to trade in an ungovernable free market.

In 1955, America was radiantly self-confident, secure in the knowledge that a free, rational society was the crowning achievement of human history. Indeed, it truly was. Our wealth and power, everything that you see around you, was created and paid for by our grandparents and great-grandparents.

Beginning in 1956, American society progressively lost her ability to build and create. Our economy switched from production to consumption, slowly depleting the vast store of wealth and power we inherited from Andrew Carnegie and J.P. Morgan, from Thomas Edison, William Shockley, Albert Einstein, Alexander Fleming, Henry Ford and Ada Lovelace. As consumers of last resort, we are partying in the fading sunset of departed ancestors.

It is not my intention to be deliberately elliptical or silly, but the next thing to talk about is movies. Two that were released in 1956 have particular significance in this context. Together, they shaped everything that America is today. They broke the stride of human progress and turned the clock of philosophy back five centuries, to a time when royalty were revered and science was forbidden.

Your television screen is proof. Today, TV brings you nothing but sports heroes and politicians, urban violence and glass-eyed evangelists, doltish celebrities and daily denunciations of science. Computer content is no better, a faithful reproduction of the Middle Ages, with gory gladiatorial VR games and limitless access to pornography. I assure you that none of this existed in 1955 and history did not mysteriously preordain that American society should slip from sanity, absent an organized conspiracy to destabilize her intellectual and moral base.

Today, Americans are living in the valley of the shadow of death, something akin to the last days of Imperial Rome, gorging ourselves on multigrain bread and digital circuses, politely avoiding discussion of the growing horde of barbarians in our midst. Our cowardice has nothing to do with lack of information. America has been muzzled by a determined (now dominant) conspiracy of thought killers.

The two films launched to destroy America from within were *The Ten Commandments* **and a science-fiction yarn** *Forbidden Planet.*

DeMille's Old Testament epic was pure propaganda, depicting Jews as God's simple, decent, oppressed "chosen people" whose faith sustained them through terrible hardship and delivered them from evil. The miracle of the Burning Bush is stupid, when you read it as fairytale words on paper, but in the workshop of Hollywood's quietly competent wage slaves, it became a convincingly "real" event on screen. The leader of the Bolshevik Revolution, V.I. Lenin, predicted that cinema would be the lynchpin of subversive propaganda. He was right. *The Ten Commandments* obliterated an American tradition of private, almost pantheistic gratitude for earth's bounty and put the Zionist myth of an angry, partisan Judeo-Christian God center stage. During the 1950s and 60s, a rash of sequels repeated the mystical claims of Judaism and Christian Fundamentalism that Jews exported to Rome. If you want a historical explanation of Jim Jones and David Koresh, look no farther than the *The Ten Commandments*. Their story is the story of charismatic Moses, leading slaves into the hand of God.

Infinitely worse than championing a literal interpretation of Old Testament hogwash, *Forbidden Planet* was an ingenious assault on science. Drawing on the theories of Sigmund Freud, *Forbidden Planet* depicted the future as a terrifying nightmare, where invisible, omnipotent demons, projected by nuclear power from the sub-conscious minds of scientific geniuses, would stalk and dismember anyone who dared to question their supremacy. It shocked America into doubting the moral competence of scientists and reliability of reason. No matter how cleverly and rationally mankind might develop itself, we were warned, the primitive "Id" of our animal subconscious will destroy us. Genius cannot be trusted. Scientific knowledge will be misused. The human mind cannot be controlled by reason or intelligence; we must submit to laws and religions, without which all the industrial achievements of humanity will be destroyed by the inherent evil of our irrational "Id."

Quite a claim, when you think about it. We can't trust reason or intelligence, therefore we should be ruled by priests and cops who never think. If you want an historical explanation of Mitt Romney and Al Gore, look no farther than *Forbidden Planet*. Romney's defense of Israel is an admittedly irrational commitment to the impenetrable claims of revealed religion. Gore's distrust of science is explicitly and repeatedly stated in U.S. environmental policy. Freedom and individual power are the last thing that Barack Obama or Hillary Clinton wants a citizen to have. It takes a village to control you.

These are the moments and the days of your life. This is the only time you have as a living, mortal being. There is no contradictory "life-after-death" where the few wise shall be humbled and many fools honored. Your freedom and happiness now, here on earth, and the freedom and happiness of your innocent children are at stake in this contest. Hollywood and Washington will use every imaginable trick to bully you into doubting yourself.

Use every scrap of your wit and ingenuity to preserve your liberty and your capacity to think. It is your right and power as a free man.

The Meaning of Liberty

Individualism is not a creed, but a fact of life.

At a crucial moment in The Good Walk Alone, when shame over-shadows purpose and regret seems like an insurmountable obstacle, Archie says: "No one has a right to your happiness except you, Janet. You are the meaning and criterion of your liberty."

The first bit seems obvious. No one has a right to your happiness except you. Emotional hostages do not grow, transcend, build, nurture, or make fresh discoveries. They are imprisoned in the past. If there is any plausible merit in Jefferson's right of revolution and life, liberty and the pursuit of happiness, surely it's an inalienable individual right to judge what constitutes one's joy and to shamelessly seek it. That's the purpose of Jeffersonian separation of church and state. If you put clerics in power, the pursuit of individual happiness is kaput.

The second proposition is far less clear: You are the meaning and criterion of your liberty. This implies a great deal, above all an inescapable element of risk. When individuals take responsibility for their decisions, right or wrong, there is no one else to blame for unexpected results. NASA didn't expect to have two Space Shuttles blow up, one on takeoff and another on re-entry, but goddamn it, they built it and flew it and were 100 percent responsible for what happened. It certainly wasn't State or Justice or Agriculture.

"Tell me why!" Reba MacEntire famously belts, "haven't I heard from you?" When our partners go quiet, something's up bigtime. People think and grow in different directions, because no two human beings are identical in spiritual-intellectual constitution. The closest we get to seeing ourselves in another is romance and intimate friendship, yet in both we are shocked at the discovery of insurmountable discords.

The best way to keep a buddy or a lover is to maintain a wide zone of privacy and tolerance. This proves incontrovertibly the existence of personal character, above and beyond our distinctions of sex, race, class, age, historical time, social pressures, best practice and oaths of office. I have four brothers, all four surprisingly unique and individual, almost nothing in common with each other except a superficial resemblance of physiognomy. DNA proves it. Five male siblings have nothing alike in their potential, aptitudes, or deficits. Their thumbprints, retinae, and histories are personal. As brothers we scarcely understand each other, like space aliens from different planets.

That's why racism is dense. In any family, group, nation, or faith, each member is an individual. That so many are intimidated by custom and ritual is a pity. That so many are driven into armies of conquest and reaction is a crime against humanity. Football fans scare me because it is so similar to war — a thuggish fanaticism of dark prehistorical origin, kicking the heads of fallen enemies around in gory desecration. Not very individual, then or now. Hitler understood absolutely the trick of emotional public events, to annihilate personal purpose and individual conscience. All prayer meetings aim at exorcism of errant selfhood.

To err is human, remember? — and I'll add, to forgive *yourself* divine. The recurring experience of every man, woman and child on earth is screwing up and struggling to recover from a blunder. We manage to do this with infinite diversity, no two disasters exactly alike. Libraries are filled with thousands of authors — Tolstoy, Fitzgerald, Clancy, Kipling — who are never confused one with another. Human life and its myriad expressions on stage, screen and the written page is absolutely personal and unrepeatable. There was not and could never be two Humphrey Bogarts, two Winston Churchills, two Ayn Rands.

That's why I say that you are the meaning and criterion of your liberty. It's unhelpful to conceive of freedom as an equal portion of an impersonal, one-size-fits-all zeitgeist. The Freeman's Constitution doesn't say anything about substantive civil rights or responsibilities, except the Article I guarantee of due process, a persistent procedural right to be heard in open court to explain yourself and your beef with an adversary, both of you presumed innocent. Presuming someone to be wrong or guilty is anathema to fair trial.

And long before shit comes to holler and everybody has to show up in court, defacto anarchy impels us to govern ourselves more or less by the seat of our pants.

The Ten Commandments cover very little and Bible study does not illuminate life on life's terms. Taken at face value 'Thou shalt not kill' nixes war in Iraq, war on cockroaches, war on bacteria, and war on beef cattle. But we never agonize over Thou Shalts or what nightmare scenario St. Paul fantasized in prospect of his imminent martyrdom. There is no holy writ that says you have to confess an awkward fact to your spouse or children, no ritual litany to recite in tempo with a pipe organ: "Oh beloved honey I got drunk with Fr-e-d-d-d and wrecked the car-r-r-r ."

Which job to take tomorrow and which to aim at later on? How much to borrow and how much to save? Is it possible to love again? Is it too late to change my mind and break free of this dreary hell, price no object? What kind of life is really mine and really meant for me? My joy of joys would be — (infinite multiple choice) — and worse, it's bound to change as one's understanding grows and explores, like a moving target.

All of these matters are personal. Courts and cops and ritual flagellation are irrelevant. We get no creative or critical thinking done at a football stadium or Sunday School. It's uniquely personal, whatever goal you choose in life, whatever obstacles arise and disasters befall unexpectedly.

The meaning and criterion of liberty is as private and nontransferable as a heartache, a work of art, a nightmare or a daydream.

Individualism is not a creed, but a fact of life.

Initiation of Force

a restatement and recapitulation of previous work

I acknowledge the existence of evil, broadly defined as the refusal to think, an evasion of personal responsibility and/or indulging fantasy instead of making an effort to gather information and apply reason.

In teaching my daughter about life, I often say it's harder to go uphill than downhill—which means: the business of study, comparison and rational thought is hard work. It is not enough to memorize a lesson in school, or to take someone else's word at face value. Especially not whatever another kid believes or says. Use your own judgment and think it through. Ask questions. If something is hard to understand (like algebra) don't despair. Take a break. Have something to eat. Go back and try again. School is a job. Learning is work.

At some point in the future, I'll have to tell her about the peril of drug use. She already knows about the dangers of parking lots, crossing a busy street, being approached by strange men, and staying up too late on a school night. I have to pay a bounty to get her to wash her hair and scrub her face three times a week, but she understands why brushing her teeth is important.

Knowledge is persuasive. Is my relationship with her consensual?

Hell, no. She had no choice about being born, and there have been countless occasions on which I ordered the kid to do or refrain from doing something, denied a request, physically picked her up despite screams of protest when she was little, and on one occasion slapped her face to stop an alarming drift toward contempt for her mother.

Initiation of force is not limited to small children. If I pass out, have a stroke, or crash my car, I will have no power to resist what's done to me by others. If I'm called for jury duty, I have to appear in court.

As Miss Rand rightly argued, the "ethics of emergencies" are false projections of the human condition and the broader, metaphysically ordained challenge of our self-directed individual progress in life. I suppose one could argue that parenthood is a continual emergency (of guardianship) that justifies initiation of force.

In 1999, John Hospers found himself puzzling in the pages of R.W. Bradford's *Liberty* magazine about something less obvious than the benevolent despotism of parenthood:

> Even with adults of normal intelligence, presumably it's all right to reason with them, or to use the force of one's personality to "work on them" to get them to make the "right" decision. But what about conning them with statements which one knows to be false? Or what about using your mellifluous voice to hypnotize someone, so that he will unresistingly agree to any suggestion you implant in him?

That calls into question the moral status of commercial advertising, newspaper op-eds, sermons, political campaigns, public education, government booklets, classic literature, movies and television. All of it is devised to 'work on you' to make the 'right' decision, and the marketplace of ideas is exceedingly narrow and deep. Wall Street is evil. Obama is good. Carbon dioxide is bad. Jon Stewart is funny.

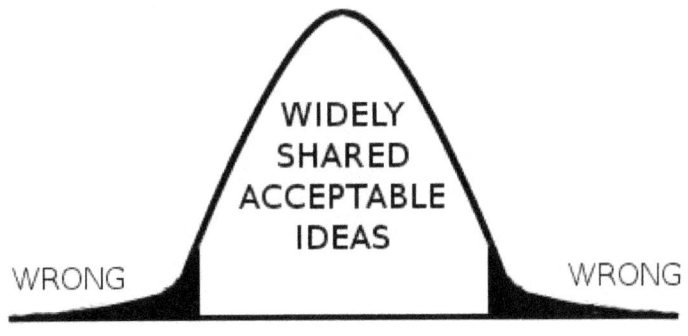

The comfortable idiocy of consensus

Within the mainstream widely-shared canon of faith, it's acceptable to disagree a little. Some people think Obama is wonderful; others are permitted to quarrel about broken promises and occasional mistakes. Nobody's perfect. You don't necessarily have to laugh at Jon Stewart, as long as you agree that television is nice. People who don't watch TV *at all* are weird. If you don't think carbon emissions are bad, there is something wrong with you.

Thou Shalt Not Be Inconvenienced

Objectivists and Libertarians, whatever else they quarrel about, are united in their moral condemnation of Initiation of Force. If you ask *why?* you get a rainbow of metaphysical and utilitarian explanations that boil down to an ordinary Boy Scout huff that *Stealing is bad.*

Thieves and thugs don't think so. They are in favor of crime. So are smugglers, pirates, prostitutes, fly-by-night roofing contractors and most of the micro-cap "oil exploration" startups listed on the London AIM and Sydney ASX stock markets. They make outrageous claims contradicted by elaborate boilerplate disclaimers that no one bothers to read. Investors don't care if there's any oil in the ground. It's a momentum play: Buy the rumor, sell the news.

High profile dopes like Ken Lay (Enron), Bernie Ebbers (WorldCom) and Aubrey McClendon (Chesapeake) pulled outrageous stunts that destroyed tens of billions in shareholder value. Bernie Madoff (the former chairman of Nasdaq) didn't steal from investors; his strategy was successful until the market turned, and 80% of the money that investors gave him was recovered. Not much of a criminal, was he?

Nor was Madoff any threat to Objectivist and Libertarian scholars, whose savings and retirement funds are safely tucked away in FDIC insured bank accounts and TIAA-CREF. Philosophical worry about Initiation of Force boils down to getting carjacked or "knocked out" by hostile thugs who roam Baltimore, Philadelphia, Milwaukee, Los Angeles and all points between, looking for soft white targets.

The "Non-Aggression Principle" (NAP) is a comfortable daydream without hope in hell of disarming the U.S. government, a local school district, or any of the street thugs you fear most.

The honest thing to do is arm yourself and defend yourself.

> The evidence isn't hard to gather, and it requires no special twist of language, no cognitive somersault. Just pick up the telephone and summon a policeman to attend a crime in progress (robbery, rape, murder, kidnapping). Good luck getting help in time. Nor is it clever to claim that the state's protection exists in a more diffuse, but efficacious realm beyond the average response time of emergency services . . . Los Angeles has 7,000 cops on duty and 7 million citizens. The LAPD are garbage collectors in fancy uniforms, picking up the dead and praying that the rest of us will argue quietly. ["Government is a Quack Faith-Healer"]

Admit it, that you are implicitly initiating force by living in a safe neighborhood and subscribing to an alarm service to guard your possessions. Admit that you know the U.S. electorate is not going to repeal the Welfare State and in fact *you don't want them to stop taxing productive households*, because you know damn fine what would happen next if tens of millions of moochers were cut off. Our cities would burn, shops looted, roads and gas stations closed.

> Big surprise, admirers of non-aggression end up endorsing coercive government. Their agenda is peace through institutionalized repression, no different than Hobbes or Hitler. ["NAP This"]

There is no way to unwind the New Deal or to reverse its destructive career. Detroit is gone. Chicago and St. Louis are next. Fifty years ago, there was a valid debate about the direction of public policy. Rand and Rothbard were ignored.

Now it's too late. Prepare for hardhearted combat.

Property

In re Cinderella

and other strange discussions from Anti-State.Com

Unless we start with a single proposition to explain all 'rights' as such, assorted provisions that seem desirable will flood over one another with conflicting application to their collective extinguishment.

> The purposes and limitations of a first principle are: (1) to establish the context and scope of discussion; (2) to affirm the existence of a fundamental truth pertaining to the topic generally; and (3) to define that truth, employing the least ambiguous and most cognitively fruitful concepts that are logically germane to the definition. Men and women have reasoned about law for centuries. Familiar terms, the relations of which are obvious in the structure of a predicate, compel any adversary to concede or to contradict squarely, because a first principle necessarily addresses a fundamental question. The most fundamental issue in law is justice -- not electoral processes or delegated powers, but the right to public justice. [The Freeman's Constitution]

>*Quote from: grounded on July 03, 2003, 09:54:35 pm*

>*Since I cannot imagine how any society could function without promises or by ignoring all promises as worthless, it seems to me that any functional legal system must take promises more seriously; implying that promises must produce legally binding rights.*

The source of law IMO is not its measurable utility. Rather, I begin with the formal purpose of an adversarial common law court — i.e., an unbiased venue to hear and adjudicate cases and controversies. Since the court cannot pronounce on the merits of a case without a hearing and many other rudiments of fair inquiry, it is logically necessary to permit any natural person or association to file a petition and be heard; to order all those named in a suit or controversy to appear and answer the claims set forth in a petition; and to compel testimony and production of relevant evidence from anyone competent to shed light on the truth or falsehood of the claims and defenses advanced by the litigants. So far, this ancap court has cost everybody time, money, and embarrassment. I don't see any inherent utility, unless it is a wonderfully wise society with judges and juries who never fail to acquit the innocent and who always award precisely fair damages. I have very modest expectations of success. Men do wrong and lie about it afterward. It often happens that there was some wrongdoing by every party in the case, including judges and juries on occasion, which multiplies the mess and creates a compelling need for appellate review. More time and money lost. So, why litigate? Most people don't and won't. They use collection agencies, credit reporting services, peer pressure, contractually mandated arbitration, or the threat of costly legal action to negotiate a settlement. I did one of these last month. The bad guy should've gone to jail, but he got off with partial restitution, which is typical of most mediation (cut the baby in half).

Does the rule of law require a state?
...or a social contract?

The rule of law has nothing to do with a sovereign state, except in the narrow sense that such states exist and when they comply with the rule of law they are viewed as 'legal persons' (litigants) possessed of competent legal standing to sue or be sued with the presumption of innocence, no greater or lesser in legal character than a single infant child. States are checked by asserting your personal right to freedom and justice – i.e., constitutional legal rights that no state may lawfully abridge. Perhaps it's a distinctly American notion.

> *Laissez faire law is discovered and demonstrated in the process of litigation and trial. It cannot be legislated, codified, or imposed by a lawgiver.* [Freeman's Constitution]

I hope that there will emerge a consensus amounting to a social contract, expressed in a constitution. But I disagree that a state is implied or inherent in the rule of law (singular 'rule of law' means you can't be punished summarily or excluded from impartial due process and fundamentally fair trial by jury).

A sovereign state's code of laws (plural) are irresponsibly decreed and altered from time to time by legislation or a single lawgiver (monarch, tyrant), making universal rules for everyone and everything. A typical provision of positive law (statute law) runs like this: Thou shalt not blank, and you are required to blank. Failure to do so shall be punished by blank.

That's not how common law courts function. In common law, there are no statutes, no fixed punishments, just A v B and their particular, often novel claims and defenses.

The way to avoid the creation of a state is simply to let go of the legal profession. Attorneys are freemen, too, you know. I hope and trust that ancaps don't intend to regulate doctors, proscribing every treatment for every patient according to NAP. It might sound good and fair to laymen "Physician do no harm" — but you'll drive able doctors out of the profession, if you make it their legal duty to heal every patient with zero uncertainty as to diagnosis or prognosis, zero adverse reactions to drugs, zero surprises in surgery.

Same thing with the common law. Lawyers have the right as freemen to argue cases on behalf of clients they choose to represent. I've suggested that lawyers should select judges, for the same reason that doctors control medical schools, certification, and hospital policy. Competition among doctors doesn't create uniform medical treat-ment, nor would common law courts foster a monopoly of legal opinion or doctrine.

The better courts and top-notch attorneys will attract the best security agencies and their competitors, but the decisions arrived at through litigation and appeal are unlikely to give much guidance to other, differently situated parties. For once, I will agree that chaos is good, or at least a measure of diversity. You need to read some case law to see that nothing in common law is readily applicable as a general rule, aside from the truly constitutional and implicit right of due process and fundamental fairness. It's rather like the adamant preference that doctors have for working in good light and a sterile surgical field.

Without stipulating the need for or desirability of arbitration as a leading institution of dispute settlement, it remains that practitioners of arbitration need a single fixed notion of their purpose and process. So, any reasoned tribunal of inquiry in the field of law requires a standard definition of justice. I am offering one that seeks the orderly abolition of sovereign states, like medicine broke free of the Roman Church with the ascendancy of secular scientific inquiry.

The right to petition and to be represented by counsel is the first and only explicit constitutional right. Justice is defined in the Preamble and mentioned often in the Freeman's Constitution, which I am sworn to uphold and defend.

Due process of law

Due process is not an end in itself. There is a principle which logically informs due process — the presumption of innocence ("Justice is the armed defense of innocent liberty"). The most important implementation is an enduring, uninterruptable right to petition the courts (Art. I), which includes habeas corpus to inquire whether someone's liberty is being wrongly denied. It might result in a retrial or outright discharge from custody, if it is later discovered that a prosecution witness lied, for instance, or a DNA sample got mixed up in the lab. These things happen. The courts have to remain open to those in custody. Persistent presumption of innocence forbids cruel and unusual punishment, and in my view ought to block capital punishment. You never know about guilty verdicts, not really. Might be brutalizing or murdering an innocent guy.

The rights of children

Children and morons have a right to be heard if they cry out within earshot of a doctor, lawyer, or extended family member. Kids and dumbbells have the right of innocent liberty from birth. Custody is not a first principle, and it is always challengeable.

Habeas corpus case: In re Cinderella, 2 DeVoon 37

Your Honor, I never promised anyone that I would care for that child for the rest of my life, and her father disappeared before she was born — he never promised me anything! — so she was sold, er, I mean married or something like that, of her own free will at the time, no matter what she says now, to a very moral extended family member in Mexico at age 14, practically a year and a half after puberty. I made a note in my diary the day she became an adult, and someone told me that she had no human rights other than those I created. After all, I'm her mother and I was here first, and you obviously don't understand this forum.

THE COURT: Her father 'disappeared'? The petitioner, who represents that she's the girl's godmother, testified that her father died in mysterious circumstances shortly after you were 'married.'

Bankruptcy and fraud

I've said nothing about the morality of bankruptcy. It is not a moral concept or issue. It's a legal matter. You cannot legally imprison or corporally punish or otherwise abuse a debtor. You cannot levy money damages in a criminal proceeding, and if damages are sought in a companion civil case, it has to be within the realm of reason. No trillion dollar judgements and orders of attachment that are tantamount to seizing every penny he ever makes, on parole or when discharged from it, for the rest of his life. No forced convict labor. No cruel and unusual punishments while in custody.

Crimes are punished by deprivation of liberty, not money damages. Civil juries can award damages, but cannot take someone's liberty (freedom to travel, accept or refuse work, etc). Equity jurisdiction can restrain or order performance in the interests of justice, but can't award damages or put people in prison, except for contempt of court (failure to refrain from or do some particular thing that they were duly ordered to refrain from or do).

Even if you sought remedies in all three jurisdictions, you couldn't tie them together and end up with a workhouse. Equity might maybe stretch to cover it, but the court would lose all independence, I think, because the benchmark in equity is fairness, not community outrage or moral turpitude as such. Overuse of equity (judicial fiat, no jury) erodes civil and criminal practice. Terrible result — a Star Chamber system of fact finding and autocratic "justice," practically Roman or canon law, instead of Anglo-American-Ancap common law. If you give judges too much power, they become tyrants. We need common law juries and strong adversarial due process. To be convicted of fraud or adjudged a debtor does not end one's right to life or his persistent presumption of innocence, nor does a verdict of legal 'guilt' appoint and constitute a complainant counterparty or lender to an office of retribution. No honest court of law will hand someone into slavery, not for any reason. Take some of his liberty, maybe. Outlaw if necessary. Empty his accounts and take his assets, sure (especially in bankruptcy). But no slaves, no taskmasters. Wrong century.

Lastly about convict labor, especially for debt. Tejano has the right take on it. Laissez faire is not Heaven or Hell, but life on life's terms. If you enter into an agreement with someone, a good judge and a fair jury will want to know if the terms were unfairly one-sided, conditions misrepresented, etc. That voids selling children into slavery.

I've criticized the Non-Aggression Principle [NAP] because (a) it doesn't provide any guidance concerning NAP-rights violations, and too many guys think it's a license to kill if they believe someone broke faith with a categorical imperative, and (b) NAP denies the existence of any legal regime other than or prior to 'non-aggression.' It's a child's view of the law: You be nice and I'll be nice, okay? No rule for bankruptcy, property, probate, or family law.

Property

I agree that anthropology is helpful in understanding the evolution of property. I believe that ancient Egypt and the Greek city-states were primarily agrarian, with pharoahs, warriors, and slaves in a stable order based on heredity or clan membership. My worry is that modern civil liberty is a weak, incoherent force and that we still rely on family and partisanship for our possession of property. There may be an exception or two in history, like the Scottish kings, who were regarded as civilian officers, not rulers. A traditional anecdote is told of newly-chosen chieftains being upbraided by a female peasant, who warned them: "If you're no good bairns (children), we'll peeble you with stains (stones)!"

>*Quote from: Hogeye on July 07, 2003, 07:01:47 am*

>*Getting more directly to the meat of the property issue: You write "Your title deed exists only in the sense that your neighbors consent to that privilege." I agree with that. But I also agree with Locke, that initial use bestows ownership. Are these views at variance? I don't think so. Even the huntergatherers understood use as a claim. Our more advanced modes of production and longer range of planning have changed things quantitatively, but not qualitatively.*

I like to think in particular cases. Does capturing a slave or feeding a child initialize ownership? If it's possible to fence an unoccupied river basin, does that initialize part ownership of the headwaters? Okay, we could elaborate a general theory with special rules (which grounded seems to prefer). But I think Lockean first use made more sense two centuries ago, in the context of unopposed homesteading. Where it never made sense was blowing off the native Americans or aboriginal Tasmanians and taking their 'unowned' lands by force.

>*Quote from: Hogeye on July 07, 2003, 07:01:47 am*

>*Moving to an important related issue: Can anarcho-capitalists and anarcho-socialists just get along? (If these two can, then combination systems such as anarcho-Georgism should be compatible, too.) It seems to me that they can if they are able to agree on or negotiate the three attributes on a metaproperty basis. By that I mean: Internally the anarcho-capitalist and anarcho-socialist societies/enclaves have their preferred system... If one enclave wants to buy land (or whatever) from another, they have to agree on the parameters of the three attributes, and also indemnify defense of the exchanged property against interlopers from their enclave. I.e., each society may run off squatters without the other society forcibly retaliating. Wolf's assertion, "Your title deed exists only in the sense that your neighbors consent to that privilege" is a statement about meta-property in the sense above. It acknowledges that even neighbors may have different notions of property, and parameters for the three attributes. Within a single homogeneous property regime, such as an anarcho-capitalist enclave, the rules are more fixed and objective. What does this mean for a jurist?*

Fixed rules (legislation) almost certainly means tyranny, unless we adopt the methods of common law to ameliorate traditional bullying by a well-armed, well-capitalized landed gentry. I suppose we could rely on stupidity as a cure, since propertyless peasants are often more ingenious than their landlords — but I specifically fear a blanket legal defense for the 'first users' and their heirs and assigns. The modern state is supposed to be a referee among contending economic classes, which Madison saw as inevitable and which became a pivotal argument in the Federalist debate. How to reconcile Free States and Slave States? How to prevent democracy from becoming socialist expropriation? How to settle conflicting land claims and protectionist trade regimes of adjacent States?

Granted, the Federalist solution was a poor one. When Jefferson returned from Paris, he was baffled by provision for bicameral lawmaking. Washington explained that it was like pouring hot tea from a cup to a saucer, to cool it. Maybe that's what happened and today's populist welfare state was slowed by decades. Senate rules and judicial review delayed the calamity of Civil War, I'd argue.

But the end of law is not to frustrate and postpone conflict. Justice delayed is justice denied. So, I ask 'Who rightly possesses this thing?' (land, improvements, roadways, rivers, children, animals) on a case by case basis, expecting that each litigant will have a novel argument that fixed rules cannot predict a priori.

In a similar way, I'm open to any theory of property that jurists can use as a reasonable maxim, if not exactly a fixed rule. Scarcity implies greater value, and creation de novo (intellectual property) seems like a slamdunk — until we consider the rule of law. If it's enforced with vigor and rigidity, based on a libertarian social contract, there will be a few smug winners and many disgruntled losers. I am particularly eager to uphold and defend the fundamental right of innocent liberty, which implies unrestricted immigration and some public property (roads and rights-of-way) to get from point A to point B unhindered.

>*Quote from: grounded on July 03, 2003, 09:54:35 pm*

>*First, one has to be convinced of the need for private property. You have to be convinced either by the economic theories of Von Mises et al, the tragedy of the commons, the history of communism or Churchill's observation "when the state owns; nobody owns and, when nobody owns, nobody cares."Once you accept the determined need for the private incentive inherent in private property, then the argument is not how the present ownership pattern emerged but, rather, how do we move forward from here.*

Well. Let's delete Hardin's theory of the commons and other extrinsic, pragmatic foundations for recognizing lawful private property. Common law is discovered by adjudication of cases. Petitioner A claims he owns a parcel of land. Respondent B in possession disputes A's claim. The judge must rule on the pleadings, evidence, and pro- cedural motions in that particular case. It may be reversible error to rely on economic theory or history, if it clouds or colors the novel and particular question of fact or law to be judged in a case. Juries are instructed to return a verdict based solely on the facts in evidence. Judges seldom have an opportunity to 'make law' while remaining an impartial referee. So, I think we're still stuck for a general theory of who justly owns what, for some reason prior to and more persuasive than unchallenged possession or possession by force.

>*Quote from: grounded on July 03, 2003, 09:54:35 pm*

>*Lawrence of Arabia persuaded and led nomadic tribes in the Middle East to overthrow their Turkish colonisers but he didn't teach them the economic value of registering land claims. Jews from all over the world purchased half of Israel from displaced and absentee Turkish landlords who did have their property claims registered...*

Great statement of a hard property case, the kind that would be regarded as exemplary legal precedent to be taught in law school, if you could get an ancap judge to rule on it. But most judges are reluctant to certify a class action. In this case, it contemplates analyzing the property claims of about 15 million people, half of whom are dead. Pretrial procedures might take a decade. Enforcement of a decision and order sounds tricky. I'm not even certain we can compel production of evidence, unless there's a profound change of heart in Palestine/Israel and a couple hundred lawyers suddenly show up in court.

>*Quote from: grounded on July 03, 2003, 09:54:35 pm*

>*Starting from a Hobbesian state-of-nature posit that the first guys who agreed "I won't mess with you and yours if you won't mess with me and mine" made the first promise which created the rights to life, liberty and property upon which foundation a whole legal structure grows by purely logical implication.*

Hmm. This is NAP restated as a Schelling point, or a custom. Common law recognizes custom ("we imbibe it at every pore") but it's not a full solution. If none of the litigants before the bar advance NAP as a theory of law, a good judge can't reach for a debatable theory of general consent that no one argued in pleadings. If the parties unanimously stipulate that NAP is their philosopher's stone, the court still can't agree to it. NAP deems all possessors to be un-challengeable and exempt from legal inquiry. NAP kills compulsory production of evidence, jury duty, execution of court orders by bankers in a civil case or law enforcement officers in a criminal case. I therefore believe it is vital to conceive law as a profession practiced by some and widely supported by many freemen who choose to exercise their powers according to a constitutional legal principle — namely, that no one should be allowed to judge his own cause of action or punish another without due process of law and funda-mentally fair trial by jury.

If ASC is representative of ancap opinion, which I believe it to be, obviously the prevailing custom or ideology is NAP, and those of us who advocate the rule of law are outnumbered by a substantial margin. This strongly suggests that the rule of law will not be instituted by unanimous acclamation. Bankers and trading networks will ratify first, requiring their customers to settle disputes in specific private law courts, probably in the context of a concise organic premise (or 'promise') that is easy to understand and to apply uniformly — in other words, a constitution. I suppose there will have to be two, one for the courts and one for a separate but comple-mentary organization to provide security, investigations, and enforcement of court orders (a constitutional Executive). The two functions should not be combined, nor do I see the Executive as a mindless slave of the Judiciary. Rather, the supreme duty of the Judiciary is to regulate and restrain the inherent power of a well-funded, dominant Executive. There is no law without enforcement and no justice without treating all parties alike. The Executive Branch is just another litigant who can be ordered to act or to refrain from a specific action.

Why would the most powerful ancap players, combined in the enterprise of a dominant security agency, choose to ratify a constitution that subordinates all of its resources and profit-making activities to judicial review? Maybe it's a utilitarian Schelling point, prompted by popular demand, after a couple more ancap experiments go bad, because some tyrant or devious cabal ran the community unchecked by the rule of law. I don't wish to discuss pending cases, but I have ample reason to say that a successful ancap community, digital or physical, must be founded on a constitution that limits arbitrary exercise of power. The town bank, the stock exchange, major employers and communication networks, especially when combined as a cartel, wield powers like a sovereign state. If there is no independent judiciary, the default is Law Merchant where the Executive becomes final arbiter of the market. No good if you want a level playing field and an impartial referee interposed between Average Joe Citizen and an insider's club of powerful market makers who audit their own books.

Defacto anarcho-capitalism exists in the world now. Perhaps as much as 10 percent of global GDP passes through the hands of shadowy outlaws and their fiduciaries. If disputes arise, they can be settled by war, or negotiation, or ancap litigation. I believe civilization thrives on the rule of law, which I often summarize as two simple rules: Don't kill each other and argue quietly (in court if necessary, as a last resort). NAP forbids war without providing any alternative venue to settle complex and profound grievances. NAP forbids enforcement of court orders, no matter how well-reasoned. NAP precludes a body of uniform family law (marriage, divorce, child custody). NAP does not tell us anything about just ownership or the obligations of a fiduciary. In sum, NAP is the death knell of all legal due process, all inquiry, all defense of the innocent who suffer at the hands of a NAP violator or a negligent drunk.

If NAP is out, if utility is debatable, and mere possession is no slamdunk proof of title (it could have been stolen and/or documents forged), what alternate principle of just ownership is there? My solution is to let ownership be decided case by case on the merits of the pleadings, with the presumption of innocence expanded to a presumption of no jurisdiction, unless someone alleges wrongful dispossession of his putative property or arbitrary impairment of his liberty.

Private morality

My wife got out frozen hamburgers for dinner. They're parked on the kitchen counter, defrosting in mute testimony to customary bovine rightlessness. Our neighbor shot an injured, suffering dog last week, and none of the local animals, kept or stray, are given much choice about reproduction. Diseased beasts are 'disappeared' as a public health matter. We use chemical WMD on cockroaches, ants, and mosquitos.

If I understand it correctly, the innovation attributed to Jesus of Nazareth was peace on earth, extended to the lame and the morally corrupt (if they repent and sin no more). Yet bugs are vilified. Some pariahs don't get any respect. We rightly regard pests as enemies, like toxic baccilli and mold. But there are few toxic, homicidal human babies or adult morons. Are they granted food and shelter by right or at our individual moral discretion? Is there a universal right to life, human or otherwise?

Well, yes, as a matter of legal philosophy. If you kill someone, he/she can't appear in court to argue his/her side of the controversy, especially a blanket death sentence, tantamount to genocide. If an endangered mosquito could pay attorney fees (or if someone cared to represent fleas and ticks pro bono), I don't know how exactly to exclude them from presumptive standing to seek injunctive relief. But I'd like to talk about something other than legal technicalities and abstract procedural rights. In "The 51% Solution" I endeavored to make it plain that moral values are not arbitrary and have consequences, the basis of which is aptly symbolized by playing cards (for instance, poker). What's laid is played. You can't undo a moral purpose, decision, or act, no matter what cards you were dealt in life. I think this helps to explain ansocs and Buddhists, plus a good deal of uncertainty that we evidently share with the bulk of humanity, including retards.

Western individualists are entitled to some triumphalism.

Communism and fascism, twin creeds of murder and "true believer" destiny, have been renounced by nearly all former adherents, except East German skinheads, the Shining Path Maoists of South America, and assorted tribal tyrannies in Africa and Asia. The world becomes progressively less idiotic, less cruel, because men learn over time that infamy carries shameful consequences.

Shame? Who the fuck cares about being named and shamed? The good opinion of others is no guide to success in self-government, or much of anything beyond an opinion poll that liked Bush one half percent better than Gore — both of whom were dumbshit standard bearers of entrenched, corrupt political dynasties with four-letter names!

Still, what's laid is played. The American electorate cannot escape moral responsibility for what happens next at the imperial White House. Likewise, an individual man is bound by consequence to his moral purpose and values. This, as flimsy as it seems, is the basis of most progress. An egoist rightly ponders outcomes. Kill and eat a few babies, your pursuit of happiness will be irrevocably expended, lost in fatal perversion and villainy. Victims are not my first concern. I worry about the mental health of ungovernable freemen, unless the function of morality is understood. I hereby certify that the law cannot catch or deter a clever evildoer. That's not the purpose of law, which exists first as a means of restraining mob violence, ignorant prejudice, and statist tyranny. If we apprehend a callous predator, from time to time, that's laudatory. But ending systemic, wholesale injustice is far more urgent, especially the heavy lifting of securing constitutional rights, which are few in number — no summary punishment, fair trial by jury, no perjury, no secret evidence, and the right of appeal to ensure fundamental fairness.

To a clever predator, who does as he pleases without fear of coffee-sipping, donut-munching lawyers and cops, I suggest a review of moral purpose. Thy will be done. If you kill babies and torture morons, you will live the rest of your days in an irreversible interior hell of your own making, a black madness in perpetual fear of discovery, which will happen sooner or later. There are very few serial killers at large, except cattle ranchers and hog producers and flag waving, stupified, weary, ultimately doomed armies of occupation. There is no ethical free ride.

Property

published by Laissez Faire City Times 1999
reprinted in 'Laissez Faire Law' 2007

In the beginning there was land and water and sky. We lived as nomads and foragers, gathering fruit and seeds where it was possible, taking fish from the rivers and game from the forest. On the great plains and parched deserts, we lived in tribes and hunted in packs, sharing whatever could be seized from the ownerless commons.

This is no paean to "the noble savage" or an approval of Rousseau's theory of general consent. It is simply a statement of fact, that our ancient roots were tribal. In a logical and irresistible way, collectivism became our first (perhaps the only) political model. Until Grotius defined an alternative during the Renaissance, the tribe was an indivisible social whole — a nation, or state, or culture — and all deeds to property were conferred by a tribal sovereign, whose voice was supposed to embody and speak for everyone.

Anticipating Ayn Rand by two hundred years, Enlightenment pioneers John Locke and Thomas Paine trumpeted the notion of individual rights (the consent of the governed). I have enormous respect for 17th- and 18th-century theories of natural equity, because our contemporary notions of ownership could not have appeared without the inspiration of Voltaire and Jefferson. It was a spiritual achievement of undeniable merit, to mentally isolate "private property" from the claims of the tribe or king as head of state.

The Declaration of Independence of 1776 created no substitute government. It merely refuted the property claims of George III. In the history of the world, there was no finer, wiser act of simple courage than the Founding Fathers' campaign to free mankind from collective servitude. Abe Lincoln and Susan B. Anthony made it real, freeing all in the name of equality. And so, the unfolding, restless American Experiment became an unprecedented model of justice that was rightly remembered as the Shot Heard 'Round The World.

Today, in every village and overcrowded city, from Russia to South Africa, people who were once ruled by totalitarian tribalism and autocratic warlords are now eagerly embracing the genteel American carrot of individual rights and private property.

Next Stop: Tyranny

They would do better to ape a train wreck, in my opinion. I specifically dispute the fantasy creed of libertarian consequentialists (and their liberal antecedents) who assert that U.S. freedom and prosperity are on auto-pilot. The 19th century was America's last hurrah — and a poor one, at that, in terms of liberty and property. The Civil War sacrificed the lives of a million Americans, ripped the U.S. Constitution to shreds, and set us against one another in a frozen paradigm of class war, rich against poor.

I don't want to waste a lot of time on history. The decline of liberty in the United States began with Republican land grants to the Big Four and Union Pacific railroad tycoons. It degenerated quickly to the

Interstate Commerce Act and anti-trust laws, regulation of employers, food inspection, exemption of trade unions from the criminal law, imposition of income taxes, and the creation of a Frankenstein fiat moneychanger called the Federal Reserve — all within two generations, immediately prior to and resulting in the Great Depression.

Contrary to textbook U.S. history, the crucial factor that saved us during World War I and II was geography. Americans were neither heroic nor blessed by advanced technology. Our industrial potential had been hobbled with senseless regulation, taxes, trade unions, and macroeconomic mismanagement. We were only marginally stronger than Germany at the commencement of World War II — and, hence, no one in the United States believed that we could fight and win a global conflict, without England at our back and France in the vanguard. Both those allies lay crushed in 1941. The only thing that kept the United States from suffering a similar fate was distance — the great oceans of the Atlantic and the Pacific — which gave Franklin Roosevelt ample time to expropriate every factory and to enslave every American worker for the purpose of warfare.

It was the wholesale sacrifice of U.S. private property and civil liberty that made us a military-industrial imperial power, able to project mechanized force across the great oceans. Our opponents were stretched thin, unable to counterattack on American soil. And so, at the end of World War II, only one industrialized nation remained intact and unharmed. Geography and curtailment of liberty transformed the U.S. into a superpower.

It is therefore stupid for anyone to wish for an American outcome, or to attempt to implement an American-style legal system of democratic government and private enterprise, no matter how dire the social conditions may be in other jurisdictions. One cannot obtain superpower privileges by undertaking Boy Scout legal oaths or grassroots political campaigns. We certainly didn't.

An Oligarchy of Power Brokers

The United States of America is no longer a free country. It is an oligarchy of power brokers, most of whom are engaged in the manipulation of less powerful nations. The average American housewife is a willing player in this conspiracy, consuming far more than she produces. Her electrical appliances, new cars, designer linens, and Disney playthings could not exist without Chinese factories and Honduran sweatshops. I am not opposed to free trade. However, the U.S. is no longer engaged in commerce, despite the flood of freight to and from Mexico and Korea. If you study the numbers, it's clear that America produces less than she consumes. Our "trade" consists of importing the agricultural and industrial output of other nations and, in exchange, exporting paper IOUs.

The world tolerates this arrangement for two reasons. The U.S. dollar is a global reserve currency, backed by military power. More importantly, the world is frightened of conflict. People will agree to anything, however unjust, provided that the Pax Americana remains undisturbed. For the past fifty years, it was unimportant that U.S. bankers and brokers arrogated to themselves a welter of luxuries (homes, cars, medical care) denied to the bulk of humanity. Most people believed that so-called "capitalist profits" were deservedly earned by American science and industrial output, acquired by virtue of U.S. ingenuity and sweat. The world could only admire or envy our success, our self-confident privilege of discretionary consumption and our Hollywood fantasies.

In reality, it was war booty, all of it. Our munitions factories drew the world's best and brightest, infusing American industry with the brainpower of twenty nations. It is surprisingly cheap to buy a man's soul. Offer him a clean house, the chance to do white collar work or to tinker with a cyclotron, and he will work gladly for a monarch. Franklin Roosevelt was a gracious, amusing king. Dinners at the White House were a riot, with Harpo Marx frequently an official court jester presiding over the punch bowl.

Nothing much has changed since then. The Clintons are no less gregarious; their Hollywood pals are no less gay—and our terms of engagement remain the same. Work for the Pentagon, live in luxury.

This arrangement is not exceptional in world history. Imperial Rome consumed more than it produced, as did colonial Spain and England. Might makes wealth. Even the hapless Soviets fared well at the expense of their subject peoples in Asia and Eastern Europe, until Moscow outspent the surplus garnered by forcible expropriation from 300 million industrial slaves.

America shares the final destiny of all imperial states — bankruptcy. At the moment, we're still riding high, because the world understands that the end of Pax Americana means global chaos and destitution. How else to explain such a fantastic nonsense, that the United States is a "consumer of last resort," giving nothing in trade except our willingness to eat? The world will agree to anything, pay any tribute we require, so long as the senators and centurions of New Rome parade on CNN with benevolent apathy, and our legions patrol the oceans of oil that keep the wheels of a transnational corporate empire turning. America has fashioned an exquisite extortion racket, happily paying a percentage to every tinpot dictator and two-bit "entrepreneur" on earth, from Singapore to Sweden, Jakarta to Jeddah, Tokyo to Tel Aviv — doling the spoils of economic rape.

New Rome on the Potomac

It is undeniable that some live in luxury, while many do not. Few enjoy actual liberty (freedom to travel), while most are indentured beyond hope of ever escaping a crowded, disease-ridden slum in Brazil or Bangladesh. I appreciate Julian Simon's thesis that the world is evolving secularly toward luxury and happiness — dramatically so since World War II, with the introduction of modern medicines and global communication. I am also mindful of Rand's thesis that what the Have Nots have not is freedom. Neither of these assertions negate the abiding claims of justice. "Property" is a corporate term today.

If you are a willing laborer for the Public Servant ruling class, you get a piece of the action – a very small piece if you are a peasant; a much larger piece if you clean toilets for Goldman Sachs. But all must serve New Rome on the Potomac, or starve.

I am not unconscious of my own collaboration with the colonels and minions of American hegemony. It was my good fortune to be born in the United States. I enjoy the privilege of accidental membership in a class of "educated," pampered Baby Boomers. Despite my opposition to the U.S. Government, no doubt my passport will be honored at any embassy or port of entry. I can enter the United States (and most other countries) whenever I please. As a stepchild of Andrew Carnegie and Walt Disney, my skillfulness as an initiate of industrial procedure and Mouse Club entertainment will always be welcome at some easy task and I will not starve, so long as I can stomach the infamy of prostitution. Americans survive, when others perish. Americans chuckle at Regis Philbin, while others rot in decrepitude. Americans want for naught, while the world labors.

It is this fundamental wrong that must be redressed — and soon — if the world is to be reborn in the light of precise reasoning, when the Great Satan of corporate America collapses, as all tyranny must.

First Principles of Value

Take the power to set you free. Kick down the door and throw away the key. Give up your needs, your poison seeds. Find yourself elected to a different kind of greed. I believe in love alone might do these things for you. I believe in the power of creation, I believe in the good vibration. I believe in love alone, yeah yeah. But won't somebody tell me what we're coming to? It might take forever 'til we watch those dreams come true. All the money in the world won't buy you peace of mind. You can have it all, but you still won't be satisfied. Money can't buy it, baby. Sex can't buy it, oooh my baby. Drugs can't buy it, little baby. You can't buy it. —Annie Lennox ("Money Can't Buy It")

Where I come from, money talks and bullshit walks. To define and understand economic justice, we need to ask what is money? Objectivists already know the canon of laissez faire political correctness — that money is a spiritual token of honesty and industry, the root of all good.

I do not fault anyone for wishing to be prosperous, hoping to shelter and feed their loved ones, their children and neighbors, to provide for their old age and its predictable infirmity later in life. We are alike in many ways. Goodness is palpable and real. The enjoyment of life is universally appealing to all sentient creatures, including dogs. Nor am I confused about the localized utilitarian benefits of mixed-economy capitalism. U.S. standard poodles eat better than women and children in the Third World and isolated parts of the Old.

Instead of discussing how many IPOs can dance on the head of a post-industrial feeding machine, I wish to examine a slightly less arcane subject. Before we can exchange tokens of ownership (money) we need to agree upon a principle of ownership. In previous writing, I suggested that the only thing a person owns outright is his or her liberty. If mankind are truly free, in a de facto sense, then no property claim can be absolute or legally negate the liberty of others. The most we can do is to possess and defend "property" by force. Indeed, this is descriptive of the world, ancient and modern. Might makes wealth. The strongest and brightest typically succeed in smothering all other claims to property and privilege, when they choose to wage economic war.

Readers who are familiar with 'The 51 Percent Solution' will understand that I am not primarily motivated by power-lust. Undoubtedly, I enjoy privileges, made richly extravagant since my wife and I moved to Laissez Faire City — but we own nothing except our capacity for action. Okay, I own my clothing in a defacto sense, because the global supply of T-shirts is such that few will wage war for possession of faded, pre-owned junk, size M. I seldom worry about the security of my reading glasses, because my prescription is personal and probably useless to others, and my passport is safe for similar reasons. How many people would wish to impersonate Wolf DeVoon?

The concept of owning nothing has a respectable pedigree. In addition to Epicurus and Buddha, it was implicitly endorsed by Jefferson, who argued "The world belongs in usufruct [for their use] to the living." He did not say that we legally owned or were capable of owning anything, but rather that the world was ours to use, to control and dispose of, without obligation to patriarchs or forebears. To hell with Grandpa. I have a right to live my own life, to wield such power as I possess to rearrange the environmental furniture. My son enjoys precisely the same right — to reject whatever I do and remake the world in his image, not mine. This is the right of revolution.

So, the problem of property is opaque. John Locke's theory is especially weak, arguing that ownership can be purchased by mixing our labor with the land. On that principle, any peasant could walk up the driveway, dig a hole in my garden, and claim it as his property. Adam Smith would probably agree. He believed that "toil and trouble" justified market prices, rents, etc. Small wonder that the world enthusiastically embraced the rabid thievery fomented by Karl Marx, since classical gurus did so little to illuminate the meaning of property.

I quoted Annie Lennox at the top of this section, because I agree with her that money (power) can't buy happiness. You can covet diamonds and jet skis – but not a pile of love. You can snort an ounce of cocaine, yet never imbibe the joy of forgiveness and grace — a deep, natural satisfaction at peace with yourself in the world. Money can't buy it. Perhaps this is why Francisco D'Anconia found it easy to sacrifice the world's oldest and largest fortune. It meant less than honor, and far less than justice. Nor was his love a marketable commodity. Near or distant, those whom we love cannot be owned by our admiration or passionate sexual desire. Approximately all we can do is to love, without bargaining.

To me, this is a vital clue. Money is fungible. If you give Israel $10 billion for a housing project, in reality you are giving them $10 billion for weapons, because they were spared a budget line item called "housing." But love is not fungible or exchangeable. My loving you gives you no love of your own. It must be generated in your own heart, by yourself, and for yourself. If you discover a value in the world, something or someone worthy of love, the recipient of your love will never be anyone other than you. Paraphrasing Ayn Rand, I swear by my love and my hunger for it, that I will never love for the sake of another man, nor ask another man to love for mine. It is a legitimate permutation of Galt's oath. We live badly without love, and die for want of spiritual food. But there can be no love transfusion, no bequest of passion or happiness — regardless of our futile whim that a vacant soul might be filled by a neighbor's joy. As Jim Morrison once shouted: You cannot petition the Lord with prayer. Love is a do-it-yourself improvement project that requires a lifetime of learning and practice.

The Game of Monopoly

For the moment, let's consider that the world is a zero-sum game, ignoring the fact that someday science will secularly lower the price of a hamburger. Five people sit down to play a game of Monopoly. You choose the racecar, and my token is the Scottie Dog. All five players announce their intention to be good sports and play fair. Since you know how to add and subtract, you are elected Banker by acclamation, and we roll the dice to see who goes first.

At first, dice rolls seem to control the game, giving some players desirable property and others a nasty tax penalty, strictly as a matter of Chance. But then the game enters its "civilized" phase, when all property has been deeded and players begin to bargain for control of Color Groups. Possession of a complete Color Group gives you the right to build houses and hotels, levying rent upon other players who (by dice roll) land on your property. It is invariably the case that someone else owns Tennessee Avenue, frustrating your possession of

New York Avenue and St. James Avenue — the two other parcels in a strategically desirable Color Group. You offer to trade two railroads for Tennessee Avenue, which seems equitable to your opponent, because that will give him a monopoly of all four railroads and increase his revenue, as well as yours. Half an hour later, you've forced a less-successful player into bankruptcy, and property is piling up on your side of the table. Life is good, right?

Not for everyone. I've sort of putzed along, half-heartedly, declining to buy much or trade anything. All I own is Vermont Avenue. I have $2 left and announce with a yawn that I'm going to my office to write, because Monopoly was boring when we played it as kids, and it's still boring. Now you have two opponents left. You fight them tooth and nail for three hours and end up the winner. Four people have been defeated, leaving you with all the paper money and property in the Monopoly universe. Well done. Now what? You gloat. Everyone concedes that you're a genius. Now what? You begin to lecture the losers on how to play. Everyone nods in polite agreement. Yes, yes, you're quite right. Thus and such were tactical errors that could've been avoided and might have prolonged the game for another ten minutes. Now what?

Dissatisfied with one victory, you enthusiastically challenge your opponents to another contest of mental skill (including me because I stupidly returned to the kitchen to pour myself another cup of coffee). We haul out a Risk board and two hundred little wooden cubes, each representing an army. For the next six hours, five people struggle for world conquest. You win. Now what?

Winning Is the Only Thing

Maybe the way to play Monopoly is with real money, taking your opponents' bread from their mouths, and when you defeat someone at Risk, he should be shot and killed like a real soldier. Parker Brothers would sell fewer board games, but the lessons imparted to children would be much clearer. To "win" means to cripple your opponent. To "lose" is to die in disgrace. It has been so forever, from Genghis Khan to Adolph Hitler and Lyndon Johnson. Undoubtedly, your destiny is to lose someday, when younger, smarter players take up the challenge and decimate the reigning champions. It happens in tennis, pro football, retail chains, investment banking, and (too often) marriages. You become a winner ... the thrill of victory fades ... trophies seem pointless ... and your trophy wife has an affair with a beach bum. It's probably happening in the Clinton household, right now. Bubba has been riding high for three decades, winning a statehouse and the presidency with dumb Good Ol' Boy Scout folksiness. Thirty years is a long time for someone to be a liar, a bag man for Tyson, and a cowardly asshole. No wonder Hillary is exploring options outside of marriage.

I feel sorry for the Clintons. After thirty years of playing hardball Monopoly, conspiring to kill people, smuggle drugs, and rob the poor, all they have to show for it is an album of family lies and bitter contempt for one another. This is no way to live, for heaven's sake. Idiots are smarter than the Clinton mob. I'm certain that no dull-witted person has ever attempted to explain a perjury by claiming that the President of the United States was a victim of child abuse because his grandmother raised her voice. It's too stupid for the stupid.

If the first principle of property is love — as Rand put it, the thing we say "yes" to, in the presence of intimate friends and romantic partners — then, surely, Milton Friedman's arbitrary tokens of exchange (Monopoly money) can't buy it. I am morally convinced that Annie Lennox and John Lennon were right. What's most at stake for a self-conscious being is peace of mind.

Sex can't buy it. Drugs can't buy it. They can help you enjoy it, if your life is dignified, honest, and gentle. But sex and drugs raise hell when consumed by a power-mad philistine like Bill Clinton. If you chemically amplify evil, the result is swaggering evil.

Anna's Holes

Perhaps the clearest received theory of property comes from a four-year-old orphan girl named Anna – commended to your attention in the short nonfiction book *Mister God, This Is Anna*. I held the movie rights to this property for several years. No studio would fund it, because Anna's life was one of the most beautiful true stories ever told. I won't attempt to explain it to you. We need only consider Anna's theory of acquisitiveness. Attention, shoppers! You are about to discover why you always feel empty, never satisfied with more new toys.

Anna's pal, Finn, wanted a motorcycle. He spoke of nothing else, dreamt about it, and was obsessed with solving the economic puzzle of how to get one. Anna explained that Finn had a "hole" in his soul, in the shape of a motorcycle — and that most people have spiritual holes. We try (and fail) to fill ourselves up with material possessions if we are incomplete as persons.

On its face, this makes a lot of sense. I don't recall that Jesus or Abe Lincoln owned anything. Ayn Rand owned very little and she didn't leave much, either. Cousin Leonard had to squeak by on backlist royalties, instead of inheriting an Objectivist Graceland and "Love Me Tender." This demonstrates the financial superiority of philistines. You can always make more dough exploiting a Good Ol' Boy like Elvis Presley or Bill Clinton than you can by attempting to educate the world on the subject of human dignity. I know from experience. It's damn difficult to make money selling moral philosophy. If Peikoff intended to milk a deluxe cash flow, he should have understudied Alan Greenspan.

The temptation of money (possession of property) is ever present and endemic. Our friends John and Marion are stuck in Scotland because it would be too upsetting for them to sell the furniture and go forward. I fully support John and Marion's comfort, if that's what they want in life. Ditto Steve and Suzi in California, Vincent and Janette in Holland, Doug and Annie in Colorado. Bless them all. Bless their possessions and their prospects for happiness. I hold the same good wishes for every man, woman, and child on the planet, including myself. This does not solve the problem of economic justice. Our preference for happiness cannot create anyone's happiness. And money can't buy it.

I know a woman who owns a 300-acre spread in a gorgeous redwood valley. She has a very limited understanding of personal dignity, because she's an heiress. The property she possesses isn't hers to enjoy, because the ranch was someone else's achievement, gifted to her by the accident of her birth. We cannot enjoy ourselves simply for being born. Although I possess an expertly sensual and healthy body, I seldom enjoy possession of fingers and toes and other faculties as an end in itself. Few are more sexually libertine or imaginative than me and Queenie, but sex doesn't give life its meaning. Drugs can't buy it. Money can't buy it. The price of human dignity is purposeful action. That presupposes a larger universe than one's infantile playpen.

Yes, you were born. Now what? If you never challenge the Unknown, you will do a lot of thumb-sucking. Winning at Monopoly doesn't change this basic proposition. With stacks of money or none, the universal question of humanity is how to redecorate your world — to take spiritual action, to surmount psychological obstacles, to dare oneself in life, because no state or tribe can live an individual life for you. You can imitate the majority, swim with the tide. But that's a cop-out. "Copping-out" means evading one's responsibility as a moral being. It specifically connotes the disgrace of treason, collaborating with New Rome on the Potomac, instead of fighting them.

It is therefore not very surprising that hippies invested a lot of time, during the past thirty years, to explore life's possibilities beyond Gucci and K-Mart. Woodstock and other tribal experiments convinced very few hippies to spend their rest of their lives as communal beggars. The concept of "private property" did not evaporate when we took LSD and saw the splendor and oneness of the Universe. What hippies concluded, after sampling everything from tofu to tantric karma, was that A is still A. Whether you own Park Place or two shabby suitcases is less important than one's inner life. It is one's private integrity that matters — not Zip codes and certainly not the profane rituals of money wealth. How many hands do you really want to shake? Bill Clinton's right hand is never still, never at rest, because he has a spiritual hole about the size of Montana that plastic smiles of social approval cannot fill. Ersatz money wealth forces him to shake hundreds of hands every day, like a circus dog on public display.

I lived most of my life in poverty — a good deal of it self-inflicted, because I kept refusing to swim with the mainstream of current affairs. Like an investment that paid off, I was recently given a luxurious home in a beautiful, exotic locale. My capacity to enjoy it is 49 years deep and as wide as the blue horizon. I have legal title to nothing and yet a fabulously rich sense of ownership. This paradox of possession must be remembered. The earth belongs in usufruct only to the living, to men and women who have filled themselves from within and have no gaping holes, thus enabling a whole self to accept the entirety of life's potential, in sickness and in health, for richer or poorer, better or worse. It's all of fortune that gives life its grandeur and challenge — not just a pile of soiled banknotes, multiplying silently in an FDIC-insured savings account or 401-k. I could not say this or ask you to accept it as reasoned argument, without having known defeat and desperate humiliation, without struggling to rise again and earn my place in the world as an integrated entity of my own creation.

Follow The Money

The precise intellectual challenge in understanding money is to perceive that 'private property' isn't truly private. As 19th-century anarchists sensibly observed, title to property cannot exist without the state. When one buys a chunk of real estate, you implicitly endorse the jurisdiction of terrestrial tribal government. Property transactions are almost impossible without money — the fungible, exchangeable, uniformly divisible tokens that are circulated as the legal tender of a powerful and jealous sovereign. No doubt, the first thing you will discover in owning a piece of the terrestrial pie is that your homestead is subject to taxation. Pay up and keeping paying or forfeit your deed. Your neighbors will most likely have rights-of-way and easements that you cannot legally renege. Your children cannot oppose public health or schooling. Even the damn dog has to be licensed and forbidden to roam, or bark, or bite. Worse: the state enjoys perpetual eminent domain for the "public good." You own nothing, citizen, and the State knows your address, if they decide to raise the rent.

Smashing the state does not end the dilution of ownership. Five kilometers from my jungle home, a bright young fellow named Rusvel owns and operates a supermarket. I spent an hour with him yesterday, explaining the rudiments of microeconomy: demand curves, prices, allocation of overhead, etc. I did this, not as a gesture of altruism, but rather self-interest. As a customer, I am an interested stakeholder. I want Rusvel to succeed and expand. His "ownership" of the store depends on my trade. I feel precisely the same way about Eastman and Sony – enterprises that I support as a filmmaker. Their continued economic success is vital to the enjoyment of my life, as theirs depends on my success.

The interconnectedness of our humanity can be described in a thousand ways, but I prefer to follow the money. Essential to the criminal enterprise of a fascist state is the power to coin money and regulate the value thereof. Finally, in the context of legal tender, we arrive at the practical meaning of property. An inventory has no value, if it cannot be traded for something that has physical utility (food, energy, transport). At present, world financial markets are rigged to secure the interests of the United States and puppet regimes in Europe, the Middle East and Asia — a ruling class of pashas and pawnbrokers, who risk nothing, consume much, and share little with those who labor to produce real, tangible goods. There can be no meaningful discussion of economic justice, unless the fraudulent balance sheet of the Federal Reserve is exposed.

In my opinion, it is incumbent upon the Third Wave militia to complete the work of Jefferson and Madison, and to liberate the money supply from New Rome on the Potomac. I never did like Alan Greenspan. We chatted for five minutes by phone, shortly before he ascended to the financial throne of a bankrupt empire, in charge of laundering Federal debt in phoney trust accounts that will never pay off. The man is a cowardly, treasonous pharisee who helped make Clinton look good. Let's fire both of them. It's not their money. It's ours.

As Milton Friedman rightly taught, the strength of the 19th-century American economy was monetary competition among private banks, each of which issued it's own "currency" of tradable notes. Competitive pressure is beneficial in the financial service sector, no less so than in other markets. If it's true that money is the root of all good — a symbol of man's productive power — it is insane to let it remain as a tool of oppression in the hands of statists, militarists, bureaucrats and tax-subsidized "industrialists" like Bill Gates, who produce nothing. The goal of anonymous cybercash, denominated in real goods (gold) is to drain loot from the looters and repatriate money to those who produce real goods.

Toward Freedom and Justice

Men are by nature territorial. All animals and plants are. It is nothing to be ashamed of, or to disparge in others. Your desire for property is good.

Unfortunately, human desire cannot produce a loaf of bread (much less a palace with a swimming pool and a backyard gold mine). To produce a loaf of bread, you must work for it. Bread production becomes considerably easier if you support division of labor, commodity trading, mining, power utilities, infrastructure development, mechanized transport, and a zillion other allegedly unrelated economic activities that contribute to efficient exchange of brainpower. Instead of baking in a charcoal pit, for instance, it's less awkward to use a commercial oven.

The point here is that we benefit from collaboration. The hungry need all of us — butcher, baker, and nuclear candlestickmaker — to exchange skills, trading value for value. Of necessity, some will contribute more value than others. Ayn Rand was quoted as saying that two percent of mankind feed and clothe the rest of us. It is unverifiable, but highly plausible that she was correct. The power of science and industry is an unearned gift, bestowed by a handful of historic men and women. If you use a computer, thank Ada Lovelace — not Microsoft.

The magnanimity of genius justifies an unequal division of property. However, it is an historical fact that people like Thomas Edison and Ayn Rand won little economic reward in comparison to their "toil and trouble." I am not able to say with certainty that lesser players in the Monopoly game of life are deserving of all the cash or property deeds piled up on their side of the table. As an anarchist, certain of de facto liberty, I tend to assume that benevolence is a hallmark of right action and that good governance inspires the loyalty of a free people who might otherwise rebel against oppression. I am not arguing for or against an aristocracy or private property, except as a natural condition, when thoughtful leadership deservedly commands the willing participation of other, less able workers. I never resent privileges bestowed upon a benefactor.

With so much wealth in the modern world, there are many who are propertied. I can't guess who earned it and who stole it from the innocent. No doubt, property will frantically change hands many times, when the Federal Reserve collapses. Perhaps the sensible thing to do is draw a line in time (when the shooting stops) and say: Enough. **Your title deed exists only in the sense that your neighbors consent to that privilege.**

Laissez faire criminal law enjoins all players to obey two simple rules — don't kill each other, and argue quietly. Property disputes will no doubt appear on the docket, with Neighbor A claiming that Neighbor B wrecked a communal septic tank, or some such rot.

I hope you realize that courts are not very good at settling such cases. Factual evidence is always debatable, and the parties to a suit are often emotionally exercised far beyond the real (or imagined) injury they sustained. People do things for spite, typically at the fringes of technical legality. In Virginia City, Neighbor A had a splendid view of the scenery. He verbally offended Neighbor B, who proceeded to erect his house smack dab on their common property line, totally blocking Neighbor A's view and access to sunlight. It was perfectly legal. Last night, someone told me an identical tale of "spite" that happened three thousand miles away and a century later in Nosara. Some things never change.

In both of those jurisdictions (19th-century Nevada and modern Costa Rica), there was very little recourse to law courts — and no violent crime. When people live in practical anarchy, they seldom attack one another, because it's too damned dangerous. The Code of the Old West was backed by an armed citizenry. Law and order hardly existed, except as an attribute of common sense.

This suggests that weak "due process" is better than a police state, if the goal of polity is non-violence. I would be happy to exclude most common law cases from court, unless someone suffered a grievous injury. We should encourage people to learn the meaning of common law by negotiating their own agreements and settling minor disputes in propria persona, instead of running to a lawyer every ten minutes, threatening suit. Attorneys should be few in number.

Interactions teach us about ourselves, so nothing is wasted by limiting legal enforcement of property claims. Intercourse is good. I recommend it especially with women, who have interesting and extensive notions about property. The arguments in favor of a female judiciary seem to gain weight and additional merit, no matter which way I turn.

As proof of this, I submit the case of Hynde v Limbaugh — one of many disputes that contract law sophistry could not equitably settle.

Rush Limbaugh sampled and mutilated a Pretenders track, "(Back To Ohio) My Town Was Gone," as his syndicated radio theme, paying a nominal royalty to a sub-licensee. Chrissie Hynde was furious that her political nemesis was using her music, and she fought desperately for seven years, using every available legal weapon to stop Limbaugh. I'm pretty sure that a female laissez faire judge – for instance, Queenie – would give Hynde instant relief and block such use of her music, on the ground of moral outrage, no matter what deal was granted to the sub-licensee. Intent matters in laissez faire law. It was never Chrissie's intent to help Rush Limbaugh.

And so, I conclude on a single point of principle with respect to property. It is not my intent to uphold private privilege to the detriment of homeless children. The right of property is contingent on responsibility — to be a reasonable, fair player in the community, reluctant to destroy the happiness of others and eager to promote human dignity and liberty. One of the simplest ways to achieve this is to offer employment, reward your employees, and quit playing Monopoly. It's stupid and tragic to die with the most toys and the most holes.

Reversed On Appeal

At dinner tonight, I asked Queenie how she would rule in the case of Hynde v Limbaugh, to verify that my prediction was correct, that a female judiciary would give great weight to "moral outrage."

Hah! The only thing I verified was my inability to second-guess the opposite sex.

Queenie ruled in favor of Rush Limbaugh, saying: "A deal is a deal. If Chrissie voluntarily sold her music to a sub-licensee, then she's stuck. She has to honor that agreement. The contract didn't restrict sale of her music to certain people, or prevent sales to Limbaugh, or Nazis, or skinheads, or anyone else. It doesn't make any difference that she and I are personal friends. Principles before personalities, bub."

I didn't dare ask what Queenie thought of property rights in general, because I sensed the distinct possibility that I might have to rewrite my entire essay. This demonstrates the solemn purpose of due process and appellate review. Next time I have something to say about justice, I think I'll write a detective novel. Book reviewers are easier to dazzle than a female court of appeal.

I know it's daft to dream about the law, instead of dealing with existential reality and immediate problems—but I like to dream. Call it professional privilege. I hereby nominate Kari Freckleton, Annie Lennox, Wendy McElroy, Mary Daly, and Camille Paglia to sit (electronically) as our first laissez faire supreme court. I trust their judgment above all. If you've studied what these five women have said publicly, as I have, perhaps you will agree that justice is safe in their sober deliberations and majority decision. If you don't know what these people achieved and stand for, I suggest you read them immediately.

The alternative is sordid and chilling—to allow Hillary Clinton, Elizabeth Dole, Diane Sawyer, Janet Reno, and Oprah Winfrey to continue to chirp in unison that everything is constitutionally peachy keen the way it is now.

Constitutional Law

Themes

Pleas

and

Documents

Saint Jim and The Trusty Knaves

Good citizens like Saint Jim are helpless to stop evil. It takes a drunk, an outlaw, a greenhorn college boy, a humorless freight driver, and a lame broncbuster who got thrown and dragged and damaged pretty bad.

Brigid did a splendid job of describing her Ideal Man — tall in the saddle, patriotic, brave, clean, and reverent. On first reading, I was miserable. I'm nearsighted, small in stature and steeped in the strong tea of Objectivism. It was some consolation that my favorite heroine also likes fictional heroes. I wrote a few on her bookshelf.

But the real deal of real life heroism is a looming shadow that nags me daily in the nicest possible way. My wife's father is an Ideal Guy. Tall in the saddle, patriotic, brave, clean, reverent, etc. Also bright as the sun, a rocket engineer by trade. A perfect father, of course. I've come to think of him as "Saint Jim" — and in fact, I admire and respect my father-in-law very sincerely. He's a wonderful man.

However, I'm bound to remark that there's a completely different star in the sky, a less-than-squeaky example of Manhood that influenced me from the tips of my fingers to the bottom of my toes, thanks to a poker-playing cowboy author named Eugene Manlove Rhodes.

How I came to know something about Gene Rhodes is a tale in itself. Once upon a time I was a minor celebrity, in print weekly with a fair sized following and a marketing hook that tempted visitors to brave the jungle for five or six hours in a speeding van driven by a tattooed Russian. The lucky ones were bundled onto a small plane.

I met them in sunglasses and sandals, bare chested and tan, with a dollar sign of silver and bone resting heavy on my sternum, just above my heart. I wore that damn lanyard two years — in sleep and awake, galloping a stallion on the beach, plowing through mud in a 4Runner, endless hours at the keyboard and modem and poolside patio. That's where I talked for a living. They came from all six continents to lounge on a hilltop, dip in the pool, and sit together at my dinner table by candlelight. The staff made breakfast and lunch, bocas and frothy pina coladas, and lobster dinner pulled fresh from the ocean that morning. The gardener was unforgettable: 80 years old, coffee colored, wrinkled and wise, with an easy laugh and bright black eyes. Nimble enough to walk up a banana tree to cut a ripe bunch with his machete and walk back down. He couldn't speak a word of English but managed to make himself understood by kinesthetic good cheer. His name translated simply and literally as "Thomas Aquinas" — a typically preposterous detail in an ocean of deeply etched memories, stranger than fiction. I haven't told you the half of it. Not a tenth, nor a hundredth.

Sorry, I'll try to stick to the subject I started with. One of my house guests scared me. He was a shaven-head kung fu instructor who flew in from icy Minnesota and had a mitten-size bandage on one hand where he recently lopped off two fingers in a snowblower.

What kind of guy sticks his hand in a snowblower?

His eyes bulged. He was big and smiley and earnest and energetic, and he was a fan, read every word of the novel I was serializing one chapter a week on the web. He had traveled 7,000 miles round trip to deliver a gift — a book of cowboy stories — a battered but carefully preserved out of print hardcover with little horses on the dust cover. And then he smiled and went home. About a month later, I opened it out of boredom.

How to explain Gene Rhodes?

He was a contemporary of F. Scott Fitzgerald and a fellow Saturday Evening Post superstar. Twice the storytelling talent of O. Henry and Hemingway put together. Relentlessly funny and intelligent, spare and authentic in a way that Mark Twain never was. A small but vital legacy bequeathed by Gene Rhodes was his love of New Mexico, the "Land of Little Rain" and the strangely literate speech of men on horseback. They smoked hand-rolled cigarettes and, as a promotion in 1910, Bull Durham sacks had a coupon redeemable in books, if you smoked enough. The books were classics. Cowboys read 'em and passed them along to each other — part of a much deeper and wider cowboy culture that shared grub and water and whatever else you needed when you rode in, whether or not the homeowner happened to be there. Cowboys carried pencils and tally books. "Ate some peaches and bacon, took your roan mare," a note might say.

Gene Rhodes' portrait of a time and place in our history as men is unequaled, fabulous. But it's only a painted backdrop; a setting that shows us wranglers and freight drivers and humorous banter as a necessary and honest Old West landscape — a range of spiritual mountains that great distances and hard, lonely work on the range night and day inspired. Men knew each other. They relied on friends and relished a chance encounter when it occurred, after weeks or months of riding alone. Every horse had a name. Cowboys sang and recited poetry. They talked to their horses.

More importantly, cowboys were good judges of men. They could size up a situation or a stranger in a blink. Why this should be so and had to be so, is easily explained. There were bad guys and train robbers and rustlers, a rifle on every saddle to deal with varmits and mad dogs. Gene Rhodes presents an immensely engaging struggle of right and wrong.

His bad guys are (and factually in Old West reality always were) crooked sheriffs, thuggish town marshals, bankers, railroad bosses, land-grabbing judges and lawyers. Rhodes also gives us sturdy deputies and more than a few honest rangers who can't be bluffed or bribed or suborned. But elected officials of every stripe conspire to steal from and deceive honest working men. Not much has changed in that regard, but life was pretty cheap in the Old West unless you could defend yourself.

His heroes? A bank robber; a daredevil fugitive from justice; a pair of pint-sized mule drivers who unravel a mystery; a cantankerous old cowboy who baffles a posse and saves a man's life by knocking him out cold; and an adventure in lawless Juarez that slams together an urbane law clerk, three hard cowboys and a smudged letter sent to a nonexistent wife from a witness to murder.

I do Gene Rhodes a disservice by squeezing his complex stories into brainless "high concept" log lines, the congenital shortsightedness of all showmen. I went through a long [expletive] song and dance with Harvey Weinstein to option Rhodes' material for the big screen. Bottom line is expiry of copyright 75 years after Gene Rhodes' death, at which point the University of New Mexico will be unable to stop anyone from butchering and rewriting a great author's gift, like Joel McCray did for Republic (*Four For Texas*) — nothing like the original Rhodes story! — an absolutely stupid waste of film.

Back to the fingerless kung fu master who gave me The Best Novels and Stories of Eugene Manlove Rhodes. He made a point of saying it several times, and he was quite right. Far and away the best story of all was Gene's slam bang morality tale of life on life's terms that I mentioned in the title of this post ("The Trusty Knaves").

Good citizens like Saint Jim are helpless to stop evil. It takes a drunk, an outlaw, a greenhorn college boy from Ann Arbor, a humorless freight driver, and a lame broncbuster who got thrown and dragged and damaged pretty bad. Together these no-account knaves rescue the cash savings of every rancher and working man in the county deposited in the town bank; bust up a conspiracy and send the bad guys scrambling, and defend the lives and property of an innocent hardworking family driving a herd to market. That's a lot of story in less than 50 pages — every bit of it brilliant and clean and calm and funny and real and thrilling as hell.

Read "The Trusty Knaves." It might not change your view of law and order. But then again it might. Like Brigid says in her profile, the militia is us. Or at least it used to be in the Old West, where men were men and carried six-shooters when they rode Home On The Range.

Justice Without Government

Consider the gauntlet thrown.

Before we fight World War III in cyberspace, let's consider why justice must be done by private individuals—not governments.

The simplest explanation is obvious: governments, as such, do not exist. Official duties are carried out by private individuals — all of whom started life as ordinary civilians, equally innocent, before they grew up to become bureaucrats or cops. I am well aware of their numerous misdeeds, exploiting the loopholes of official discretion, while wielding the practical power of armed supremacy. This is an additional reason to frown, when someone says that government is a necessary or desirable form of social control. But the central bone of contention, throughout the centuries, was *not* whether individual magistrates acted properly in aid of liberty and justice, but rather whether there should be created and maintained a class of men to govern other men, typically a few in power over the many.

In answer to this question, liberal fundamentalists (anarchists) shouted *No!* while thousands of effete scholars whimpered *maybe*, claiming to discern the public weal in a kaleidoscope of buts and howevers.

The Liberal Agenda

If it sounds odd that I describe myself as a liberal, there is really nothing mysterious about it. "Liberals" (as the name implies, and as I use the term here) are in favor of liberty – not for the few, but for the many, as of right. Fundamentalists take it seriously. As children we soaped the neighbors' windows and experimented with fireworks. As teenagers we fought turf wars or committed other crimes. Now adults, we recognize no collective authority, the legitimacy of no one to be King or Commissar over an unarmed, subservient, terrified peasant class.

Most anarchists are former peasants. We found it necessary to experience the tense drama of law-breaking, in a social system built on lies and infamy, which impels men to cry: "Smash the state!"

Statists on the other hand never break the law. They are employed at state universities, nonprofit think tanks, and tax-exempt political orgs. Nothing is more important than their next salary and benefits package, regardless of whether liberty waxes or wanes for the many. If the economy tanks, Cato will feel divinely anointed to reason with the functionaries and flunkies of state. But they will never put their butts on the firing line and man the barricades along Pennsylvania Avenue. It is inaccurate to call them chickens. They are traitors and collaborators—modern Tories—who are ideologically married to and financially in bed with the sovereign. In 1770-76, their political ancestors' estates were confiscated and their homes were burned by the Sons of Liberty. *Sic transit gloria Cato*. If your name appears on a libertarian email list, have it deleted immediately. The only safe place to get information about the future is Laissez Faire City.

The information you need is simple. You are a free individual, with no obligation to anyone else, as a first principle of legal philosophy and an observable fact of life. Liberty is the cornerstone of justice.

Due Process

It is important to understand that there is no way to do justice wholesale by legislation, municipal elections, etc. Justice is always done retail, one case at a time. It is done deliberately and slowly. Was that witness telling the truth? Is this document authentic?

It is every person's job to judge the facts of reality, separating truth from falsehood, right from wrong, giving each man his due. Some men deserve our loyalty and service. Some must be punished. We, each of us, do this privately, choosing lovers and friends on their evident merit, shunning others because they are evil assholes. It is particularly confusing when the asshole in question is a family member (spouse, child, parent). But justice excuses no one.

If dad is an asshole, he should be disowned. There are plenty of good men among the Six Billion to take his place in your sentimental scrapbook of 'family'—a term in the color-blind language of justice that refers universally to every man and woman in the Family of Rational Beings, past and present. It is specifically evil to exempt someone from justice because he is a blood relative. Justice is thicker than race, religion, or kinship. The notion of divorce exists because your liberty cannot justly be held hostage by a spouse. If your kids are brats, they deserve wrath — not Tootsie Roll appeasement and a smile of paternal indulgence.

Although it was 25 years ago I remember them still, a little knot of tipsy, gregarious law students in a State Street bar. They were partying, soon to graduate from UW-Madison's reputable school of law. Equally intoxicated that night, because I spent the day reading history, I bellowed a question at them: "What's the opposite of *justice*?" They hemmed and hawed. A boy giggled 'injustice'. But the brighter kids guessed that there was an answer that could change their lives and careers, if they had the courage to listen. "The opposite of justice is *mercy*!" I hectored (echoing Ayn Rand).

We do mercy at our peril. If this is not obvious to you, then you have not been given much responsibility. Every boss, every banker, every Boy Scout leader and kindergarten teacher knows what happens if you let an evildoer get away with some small transgression. Suddenly, he wants to commit big ones — and it's harder to stop him, because he was exempted from justice on a previous occasion. The question of public policy, no matter how abstruse or boring its object, is whether or not to do justice.

The job of enforcement is done by all of us and each of us, every day of the week, acting as civilian judges of one another in our immediate society. When we meet a new acquaintance, the verdict pronounced on a pal is innocent until proved guilty. When we angrily ridicule the Clinton mob, our judgment is 'guilty beyond reasonable doubt' — but guilty of *what*?

Obstruction of Justice

Of all the accusations hurled at Bill and Hillary, only one condemns their stewardship of the Federal government as criminally wrong — willful obstruction of justice while acting under color of law. It is extremely difficult for an average citizen to obstruct due process or faithful execution of the laws. Government officials are the only ones who can frustrate public justice by pulling strings behind the scenes.

Corruption is such a toxic threat to due process that many anarchists believe we can't trust anyone, ever, to wear a badge or wield a gavel. I disagree. I have argued vigorously in favor of private law courts and public law enforcement. See "Principles of Internet Law."

Justice cannot be done by inaction, or whim, or prayers for divine intervention. The bad guys must be stopped — it's as simple as that. Objective public justice is a difficult, painstaking process, aptly dramatized today in Dick Wolf's *Law and Order* series on television.

Judicial corruption is not my first concern, nor is it much of a threat compared to widespread suburban U.S. support for tyranny. Judges are seldom better than the nation they serve. Given the existence of an imperial state, which has monopolized law to control an overfed, lethargic society, it is a miracle that U.S. courts still strive to preserve the rudiments of due process. This demonstrates the ancient if unarmed, feeble power of law courts to promote liberty and justice. Nothing is more respectable or fearsome than a fair trial by jury in open court with rigorous rules of evidence and competent counsel free to debate the guilt or innocence of an accused. Prof. Juhasz is dead wrong on the facts: American jurisprudence is not for sale to the highest bidder. Despite a century of perverted legislation, adversarial due process is still better than any Napoleonic tribunal of state inquisitors.

As a novelist, my job is to write about abstract values. Courage. Romantic love. Human dignity. Once in a while, I use the device of exposition to summarize the meaning of events.

In Mars Shall Thunder, the following passage explained what I know about the rule of law in America:

"Human beings are a funny bunch. Put a flag in the corner of a room with The Great Seal staring at down at them and something moves inside, like a switch that says shut up and listen. You didn't create this. It was bought and paid for by a pantheon of patriots and simple, decent men who sacrificed their lives, long before you were born. It is the source and root of whatever you cherish in life, the food you eat without stopping to ask how it came to happen, that our lives are richly endowed by machines and technological conveniences denied to every living species in the universe, except the ones who have law. It follows us like the air we breathe, in every waking moment, every transaction with our kith and kin. When a kid says 'It's mine!' he's talking about property. When his mother says 'No' to a fast-talking salesman or a preacher, she's defending the notion of civil liberty. And when two drunks square off in a pub, the only barrier to mayhem is law and order, sometimes in the person of an innkeeper, but just as often another drunk, a citizen, who invokes the letter and spirit of polity when he yells out an injunction like: 'Hey, hold it down!'

"Sometimes, getting people to shut up and listen is the whole enterprise of government. Disputes are common. Settlements require a ceasefire and enough patience to speak calmly and rationally, both sides, one at a time. From time immemorial, long before our written history as a people, there were courts, where combatants and petitioners had to shut up and listen if they wanted to find an equitable solution, so life could go forward."

World War III

Yes, I am a patriot. It is not wrong to be an American patriot, if your love of country pertains, not to the present, but to the historic achievement of the Founding Fathers, who fought for justice and freed themselves from tyranny. I am humbled to be an American patriot, and I hope I have the wit and courage that patriotism requires, because Jefferson and Madison were animated by a lifelong passion for justice. It is rare to hear it said by lawyers today, but in colonial America the question of "liberty and justice" was a single problem, admitting of a single remedy in 1776 — the American Revolutionary War of Independence.

On the eve of a digital war of independence, it is my duty to caution that chaos advances nothing—and cyberpatriots will probably inspire more public disorder than at any previous time in history.

It is a mistake to assume that World War II was a time of terrible chaos. Far from it. Italy, Germany, France, Russia, Japan, and the Anglo-American democracies were cohesive societies led by charismatic officials, who mobilized entire nations without much dissent. While it's true that governments forbade dissent and punished it, the temper of the time was obedience and selfless service to society. In Germany, that meant the Fuhrer. In Britain, it was a Royal Empire. Americans fought for the New Deal and apple pie. Such abject mass submission to monolithic authority no longer exists, because WWII governments were the most viciously sacrificial and murderous in all of recorded history. Their last hurrah was Vietnam. We said 'No!'

The blackjack of genocidal government hangs over us, threatening to use nuclear weapons as a last resort. It is a bluff that will be called.

In Russia, command and control of the army is doubtful. In Pakistan and India, the struggle for a mountain province could trigger annihilation of millions of people and toss the subcontinent back to a prehistoric condition, where wild beasts roam through a smoldering holocaust in search of human remains. In Red China, the temptation is building inexorably to invade Taiwan and square off against the U.S. Seventh Fleet. The final recourse available to Israel, against Iraq and Iran, is a hydrogen bomb.

It is in this circumstance of terror that some now propose to sabotage the world economic system — to destabilize the financial infrastructure of a global civilization. There is no soft option. There is no 'kinder, gentler' means available to us. As the New Hampshire motto factually states, we must live free or die, because justice cannot be sliced like a carrot. Men are not garden vegetables, to be harvested for the benefit of tax collectors and their fraudulent pension schemes.

The Defense of Right and Reason

The most dire threats will be made against us. Every branch of tyranny will attempt to put down the Cyber War of Independence. In the chaos that ensues during the coming years, each man and woman will have multiple opportunities to do individual private justice. The fate of the world will be determined by your choices. If you collaborate with tyranny, you increase the likelihood of another Hitler's rise to power — this time, an American Fuhrer (George W. Bush, Al Gore, Pat Buchanan) whose military and police powers have no equal in the world. If you resist U.S./EC internet regulations or FBI/MI5 wiretaps, they will brand you as an outlaw.

So, I turn to Churchill for inspiration, the last of the great Liberals, who saw liberty and justice as a single problem with a single solution. "It is vain to imagine," he warned, "that the mere perception or declaration of right principles, whether in one country or in many countries, will be of any value unless they are supported by those qualities of civic virtue and manly courage — aye, and by those instruments and agencies of force and science which in the last resort must be the defense of right and reason" (address to the University of Bristol, July 2, 1938).

To defeat tyranny in cyberspace, it is not enough to stay home and fill your cellar with carrots. History beckons you to help do justice, by punishing those who would steal your liberty and rewarding those who are about to risk everything as patriots in battle. Cyberwar will not be fought with bullets or bombs. It will be a contest of ones and zeroes, draining strength from a bankrupt Global Superpower—the end of which is liberty for all, freed from the charade of social security. The core purpose of liberal values is not charity. LIBERTY is a constant, inalienable responsibility to choose friends wisely and to drop them if they betray you. JUSTICE is the action required.

The United States Government has exerted every talon and claw to keep the mall stocked with playthings, to expand TV into a thousand channels of trashy circus, and to postpone the inconvenience of you personally governing your own life. Like pulling on a rubber band, loading potential energy into an economic slingshot, U.S. public servants have postponed justice for 50 years. Time's up! — wave goodbye to Mickey and Donald and Goofy. America is going to grow up, whether we want to or not. A digital genie escaped from the military-industrial Establishment into the keystrokes of freedom fighters. This is a proof of *defacto* private justice, that human genius worked to the advantage of all men, not just the few in power.

It is my hope that soon, and with a sense of urgency, there will be begun a sober debate about the need for new institutions — not government as such, but a continuation and improvement of the rule of law. I have said as much as I can on this subject. It's time for others to join in the work, to define and provide mechanisms of due process in a Free Society of equals, where the legal notion of sovereignty pertains exclusively to individual men, women, and children.

But I will say one thing more on the subject of liberal justice, because it is important to mention compassion and forgiveness. I hereby pardon those who tried in good faith to 'work within the system' and celebrated liberty as an American tradition — the Libertarian Party, Reason Foundation, Cato Institute, Hazlitt Foundation, George Mason University — provided that they renounce the validity of the state. Justice includes the notion of rehabilitation, until escalating commencement of hostilities makes it difficult to forgive anyone stuck in the middle ground between liberty and tyranny.

Consider the gauntlet thrown.

Capitalism

excerpts from an article published in 1998

"Capital" means capital plant and equipment. When it's time to cut a bar of steel in half or punch a tunnel through a mountain, all the haircuts, sovereign debts, central bankers, and newspaper columns in the world can't do it.

However decorative and amusing Disney movies, tourists, sportsmen and priests purport to be, in reality consumption contributes nothing to the work of production. Whether the capital in question is a paintbrush, or a petrochemical plant, or an oil rig, or the pipe-welding robots and steel mills that make it possible to exploit a naturally inaccessible, dangerous, useless raw muck, the productive power of tangible investment in the form of industrial plant and equipment is the literal (and largely forgotten) basis of capitalism.

Before you can have a market, you need goods. Pieces of paper and taxes are not goods; they are merely claims to goods.

Let's talk about actual physical goods: food, clothing, shelter, energy to keep us warm in the winter, mechanized transport, medicine and sanitation. These are tangible, life-sustaining physical goods that free societies enjoy in great abundance.

We need to look at capitalism from a simple, proletarian perspective — at the level of nuts and bolts and seed grain. Free enterprise rewards study, forethought, frugality, fidelity, intelligence, initiative, willingness to experiment, and showing up for work every day, ready to work whether it's fun or not. This is the reality of work, whether the work is skilled or unskilled, physical or mental. Most employers recognize and reward productivity. It is in their interest to recruit and retain able, hard working people. No employer deliberately hires lazy sycophants and stooges.

— except in government. Political office rewards conventionality, seniority, multiple meaningless rituals, symbolic gestures, half-truths, evasions, deliberate delay, trading the unearned, shaking hands, smiling, empty platitudes, feigned concern, absolute allegiance to the party line and the party leader, secret deals, backbiting, paranoia and showing up at cocktail parties to beg for money and favors.

Capital plant and equipment is the lifeblood and sinew of private enterprise. The vast bulk of productive investment is NOT financed by the so-called "capital markets," nor from government handouts or tax breaks, but instead from retained earnings.

Proper maintenance of plant and equipment is a crucial priority for every factory, every farm, and every pilot of an 18-wheeler. Freedom implies responsibility. If your competitors have better technology, they cut costs and win customers. The free market economy is a school in permanent session, teaching every participant the virtue of practical education. We don't always enjoy learning to use new tools — but we do it to stay in business and to make ends meet. Until very recently, the secular trend across all industries throughout American economic history has been falling prices and rising productivity. The computer on my desk cost $1000 and quietly outperforms any $1,000,000 mainframe built 30 years ago.

None of this applies to government. The bulk of state investment is NOT obtained from its operational revenue or taxation, which barely cover the salaries and pensions of a constantly growing number of government drones. Badly-timed, over-specified, bloated investment in state plant and equipment (weapons, office buildings, roads) are funded by the one and only "capital market" that governments care about — sovereign bond auctions.

US bureaucrats, legislators, military planners and school districts have no incentive to maintain their plant and equipment. Dependence implies irresponsibility. Whether you view the government as a recipient of our willing charity, or as a thief who holds taxpayers at gunpoint, the essence of the game is dependence.

Government makes nothing, sells nothing, earns nothing. Their entire strategy is to elaborate and expand governmental operations, preferably to do less with more.

Social Security and Medicare are out of control, suffering the same fate as Britain's NHS, for the same demographic and technical reasons. A Ponzi pyramid cannot succeed by robbing Peter to pay Paul, with increasing numbers of idle Pauls and an eroding number of taxpaying Peters. These are well known facts. There is no known solution, except to face the facts and confess that we have too much government, too little liberty.

Liberty is a profoundly unpopular idea. Throughout the world, terrified bankers and stock brokers are whimpering their conversion to Anatole Kaletsky's faith. "What is certain," Kaletsky assures them in confident, fatherly tones, "is that the era of laisser-faire ideology is fading. Capitalism's own incomparable instinct of self-preservation will see to that." [London Times editorial, September 10, 1998]

My hammer and nail have an instinct of self-preservation? — even if I leave them out in the rain, or give them to a starving Haitian? This is what happens when you stretch an abstraction to the outer limits of anthropomorphism.

What many people mistakenly call "capitalism" is the intangible financial services conducted by intermediaries who trade claims to wealth at varying dates and terms of payment. In J.P. Morgan's day, it was called banking. It's the pixie dust that allegedly pulled America into a healthier and happier service economy. Because it has no furnaces, factories, or chemical effluents, it is 100 percent eco friendly.

Like the government which regulates financial services and enforces debt contracts, banking is inert of productive power. All the bankers and brokers in the City of London couldn't make a ham sandwich without help from farms, factories, oil wells, refineries, power plants, transportation, butchers, bakers, and nuclear candlestick makers.

Walking to Ayrshire

"Fuck everybody else."

Life is a spiral, I'm told. You curve up or down, swing around and see the same, familiar sights. I used to do this whenever I went to Wisconsin. Got tired of it, don't go there any more. In rebellion, Wisconsin follows me around the spiral. My brother surfed the web until he found my attorney and obtained an address in Scotland, where I've been hiding. Families are like public confessions of bad behavior. They never go away, not even if you disown them. I'll have to change my name.

But before I do, I want to settle a few accounts.

I owe you nothing. Not my time or concern, not a gram of happiness or energy. Your misery and vacuous pretenses are dreadful to behold, much less celebrate. I don't even feel contempt for you any more, after five weeks of competent psychotherapy (a rare combination bestowed by luck, after walking to Ayrshire). I'm finally free to say goodbye. And it doesn't matter whether the goodbye pertains to Wisconsin or CBS or Israel — I'm outta here, gone to Mars and I ain't comin' back.

I don't care any more about the destiny of others. Anarchy is pure democracy, without the opinion polls. Feel free to experiment, minus me.

I don't care any more about justice. I'm satisfied that justice cannot go out of existence. It's manufactured by consequence, implicit in every word and deed. It's deaf to our dissembling lies, except as a bullshit detector. Motives are nothing. There are five billion people in the world, with five billion dead and five more on the way. If you feel entitled to take hostages, try taking somebody else. I don't want to play. My loyalty is to myself from now on. If you force the issue, I'm prepared to fight for freedom and I have no inclination to fight fair in defense of liberty. Consider yourself warned.

This is what happens when a person walks to Ayrshire. The fresh air of absolute freedom cleared my head, so I could think straight. And since you probably don't know where Ayrshire is or what walking there might be like, I'll explain. I'm a writer. I explain things for a living, whether you understand them or not, whether I get paid or not. My living is in the writing. After that, it's up to somebody else — and I don't give a fuck any more about publishers or readers, because I walked to Ayrshire.

For forty-seven years, I wanted to make my way in the world, I wanted the same things you want. Integrity. Success. Love.

Not any more. I don't care whether my integrity is measured in feathers or inches. Success looks like a pile of shit, as far as I can understand it, because it involves treating Jay Leno like an intellectual equal and serving the purpose of light entertainment. What kind of "success" is that? And love is too precious to waste. God knows, I've thrown it away by the barrel, squandering it on friends and family, girlfriends and wives, children and abstract ideals — without much return on investment. The fastest way to alienate a kid is to pour buckets of love and affection on his or her empty head. The best thing I've done with Buffy is to give her nothing, rigorously trading value-for-value, like competitive shopkeepers.

But nine months ago, I was bankrupt — partly from squandering my love on others, but mostly from eating the junk food of moral integrity and perpetually hungering after commercial success. We were stuck in a single, uncomfortable bedroom in a pitifully boring village on a Scottish island, cut off from the world as completely as two professional communicators can be. I applied for 50 jobs and got nada. The People's Republic of Scotland gave us a weekly allowance for food. We had nothing else. No prospects, no ideas, no energy to go forward. In case you don't understand what moral bankruptcy is or feels like, try sticking yourself in somebody else's closet for five months, squashed behind their golf clubs and old tweed coats, a bare bulb for illumination and nothing to read but the King James Bible. After a while TV starts to look interesting. Then TV becomes important and you know the schedule by heart. That's moral bankruptcy.

We quarreled (about which program to watch) and it escalated to moral divorce, no further business to transact, because I was bankrupt. I took £5 from the sugar bowl and packed an overnight bag, consisting of two shirts, a toothbrush, my passport, and four pairs of clean socks. She demanded that I take off my wedding ring.

I refused. Moral bankrupts get to keep their love, especially if it's unsaleable, I mumbled. Nothing further to say to each other, I walked down to the ferry on a brisk August day and splashed to Gourock, a maudlin journey of about twenty minutes. After fifteen years of partnership, it's lonely to travel by yourself, especially if you don't know where you're going.

I thought I was headed back to the States, maybe to Hillsdale College to get a job as a janitor or short order cook. It didn't matter. And I didn't feel very confident. About the last thing I wanted to do was to fight my way through Glasgow or hitchhike on a freeway. I didn't want anything from anybody, except a plane ticket courtesy of the U.S. Government. Citizenship has its privileges, I imagined. So, I started walking in the direction of Prestwick Airport, following the coastal road from Gourock to Ayrshire. This made about as much sense as diving off a pier.

Prestwick Airport was 50 miles away. I stopped to buy a pack of cigarettes, and I remember thinking that I still had a surplus of £2 for breakfast, so I wouldn't starve. It was four o'clock in the afternoon when I draped my travel bag over one shoulder and started walking to Ayrshire.

No matter how far I walked that afternoon, the seashore village that I left kept glaring at me across the Firth of Clyde. My wife was over there, and I had no right to go "home" any more. The room that we shared in dull poverty was warm and comfortable, compared to a lonely, windswept coastal road.

Big square houses dotted the footpath and then disappeared. I had to cross over and shuffle through the gravel, cars whizzing from behind and thumping against my senses, as their shock waves cut the quiet stretch of narrow road. Maybe it was rush hour in the Middle of Nowhere, because there were a lot of cars, driven angrily and too fast to hold their grip on a lumpy, rounded chicane. They screeched through blind corners, tempting fate to put their occupants out of some complicated operatic misery that I could only guess at through tinted glass. My eyes are pretty sharp. I saw the stuffed toys and Kleenex, the fat ladies and screaming kids, the cellular handsets and scowls of frustration.

Once in a while there was an empty bus, a massive 18-wheeler, a motorbike, or a camper full of plastic and propane. But mostly it was black, curvaceous Fiats and Beamers, racing past a troop of make believe cousins. How Europeans can overtake two or three cars on a blind corner always amazes me. Walking was safer — even walking on the berm of Death Race 2000, where curly daggers of gorse and thistle kept me inches from the next fender. After a while my ears were like radar. I could hear a car coming and duck into the next gap of gorse, step over the steel barrier and wait for him to whiz past, flapping my black trenchcoat in the jetstream. For now the sun was down and my lighter-weight jacket was as comfortable as bare skin in the freezing darkness.

If you get bored, try it some time — walking along a narrow strip of gravel at night, wearing a black trenchcoat and dodging the macho mechanized lunatic fringe of European mediocracy.

Boy Scout rules of the road don't apply in such circumstances. I tried walking on the side facing traffic and got nowhere. There was a solid wall of steel and tall prickly hedge on that side. No sooner had I pried myself loose and stepped into the road, than another convoy of death forced me back again, face buried in sticks designed to repel trespassers like me.

Some miles later, the other side of the road gave out, and there was nothing left to walk on. The narrow band of racetrack was busier than ever. Down I went to a rocky shore littered with pebbles and boulders, not much better than an obstacle course on the dark side of the moon. Crumbling cliffs gave underfoot, soaked to a jelly by tide and rain, a plentiful natural resource in Scotland. Then the shorefront ended, roadway cutting me off in a strategic sweep to the sea. No pedestrians, it announced with a sniff of dim indifference. I had to break a trail through iron thistle and gorse if I wanted to get up on the road again. Looking back, I could see a meandering swathe of anger, about two feet wide, where somebody my size refused to follow instructions.

The next six or seven miles were the worst. I knew I could be killed like a bug on a windshield, so I didn't have a chance to do much theoretical speculation. Car coming, dive for shelter again.

There was a town, finally, and the luxury of sidewalks. Women walking their dogs in a park, eyeing me with suspicion. Calm, solid houses with flashing blue TV windows — all nice and legal. I remember the streetlamps and gutters, things that seemed mine in a world of theirs. The road took me to a busy downtown with brazen, noisy crowds laughing in restaurants and bars. No public restrooms, no water fountains. Stuff that begins to matter when you're homeless and too ashamed to beg.

I made a big mistake in Largs. I should have refilled my water bottle, instead of hurrying past the jubilee of conspicuous curbs and stoplights. But it was getting late, maybe nine o'clock, and I was tired. We don't always make good decisions tired.

Like all signs erected at public expense, it misstated reality, pointing to a public park and a scenic view thataway. Sounded good, far enough from civilization to sleep in peace, without being roused by the cops — so I hoofed it up a winding country lane that wove through a forest of soggy leaves, dodging a stream of creative commuters who bet their buddies a quart of vodka that they were still sober enough to drive. Two miles up, the hill finally crested in a barren, flat gale-force wall of stinging raindrops.

At the summit of this walk-in wind tunnel, there was a trash can, a picnic table, two bushes and a fence. Fine. Whatever. I was too tired to argue. I fished around for a clean pair of socks and made a pillow of everything else, tucked under a breezy shrub that was less wet than elsewhere. Maybe I slept. But it's hard to sleep when you're freezing cold and it's not very bright to court hypothermia.

A few minutes later I was back on deck, staggering back down a winding mountain road that I should never have seen once. Walking to Ayrshire was beginning to have the desired effect. I felt like a mis-wired robot, trudging through a cold, windy rainstorm that opened up like a cheap umbrella and blew away. A few confident stragglers in big black Mercedes flew down the highway, while I stopped to cower in the lee of a stone wall and the worst of the storm drenched the air, turning it sweet with ions. Maybe it was midnight.

Miles later, there was a bicycle path next to the road. Fine. Thank you. It idly curved away. Whatever starlight had been guiding me was suddenly gone in a thicket of tall trees and rustling bush. I was far enough from civilization to qualify as prey. The only weapon to hand was a Bic lighter, so I picked up a rock. My footsteps went stealthy and once or twice I had to freeze, to let radar ears and x-ray eyes operate at full range.

But it finally occurred to me that it made more sense to walk like a man, make noise, dare 'em (lions and tigers and bears) to do their worst. In a sliver of moonlight, I saw a baby frog hop onto the path in agreement.

This went on approximately forever — past a nuclear power plant, covered in big florescent lights, conveniently situated in endless miles of nothing and no one — until the first gray pallor of dawn brought me to a roadside diner, British cuisine at its best. I had to wait an hour or two, stamping my feet to stay warm until a pimply-faced kid arrived with a key that he hated as much as his dreary job.

There was something resembling coffee and eggs, half a bath in the sink, my dead shirt thrown in the trash and another clean pair of socks. But the damage had already been done. My feet were covered in gigantic blisters that couldn't take a normal stride. Walking to Ayrshire became a hobble at half speed.

I guess it was noon when I limped through Irvine, a fairly big city. I tried to find a police station, thinking it was time to ask for help. I looked like shit and, given a thick enough audience, I could improvise a fair impression of lunacy. I stopped a kid on the street and asked directions to the nearest barracks. He didn't know.

The din of city traffic kept me moving against my will. Yards became miles, and the city finally ended at a freeway on-ramp. Unable to walk another inch, I pulled out a piece of paper and a black Sharpie, stowed in plastic for just such an emergency. I traced the letters carefully in drop-shadow, big enough to be seen from geostationary orbit: Prestwick.

It was only nine miles away as the 18-wheeler flies and, sure enough a big one carrying odorless, colorless white bread promptly scooped me up. I limped into the terminal and asked to see an Immigration Officer. He was odorless and colorless, too — but kind enough to contact my embassy and bring back the bad news. Americans have no right to go anywhere at government expense. Worse: getting kicked out of marriage to a British citizen confers the legal right to remain in Britain and receive free food and shelter, unless you commit suicide. Neither of these plans sounded very good.

I was dead tired, practically unable to keep my eyes open. I couldn't walk in any meaningful sense of the term and my shoulders were covered in bruises from carrying an unruly, lopsided bag. I wasn't merely unemployed — I was unemployable and finished with the world of commerce. And I was stuck to a hard plastic bench in the middle of Prestwick's empty ticketing hall, having stumbled 50 miles to the only airport on earth that doesn't fly people anywhere (it's a cargo and charter operation). If ever there was an opportunity for me to "gracefully surrender the things of youth" it was at Prestwick, listening to the drone of elevator music and staring at the layout of ceiling speakers that I would have certainly designed differently. It was time to surrender.

I said goodbye to the intrepid kid who went to prison and hung out with macho Puerto Ricans in Philadelphia. I said goodbye to the guy who showed Lockheed how to fix the L-1011 cockpit windscreen. I said goodbye to the artist who told Hollywood and Paris to shove it up their asses sideways. I said goodbye to everything I ever thought or believed, everything I knew and loved and wanted to keep.

It took a while to figure out how to use a telephone, but I got through to Buffy and asked her to come and get me. About four hours later she got there, gave me some food and took me home. I had to stay in bed for a week before I was strong enough to see the family doctor and explain that I had done something highly irrational, walking to Ayrshire. He referred me to the NHS psychology clinic.

After six months on the waiting list, I went to meet an intelligent stranger and told him what happened. His advice was succinct and to the point: "Fuck everybody else. Finish the novel."

I had never before taken advice from another human being, because I saw myself as competent before I walked to Ayrshire and proved otherwise. Now that I've resigned, I feel considerably better. The unpublished novel is unspeakably beautiful and right.

No More Mr. Nice Guy

Get off your ass and smash the state.

If you believe that our dream images are significant, here's a doozey: I saw myself emerge from an egg-like membrane, physically transformed in a new shape, with new powers, ready for battle. In the morning before I had a chance to mention this dream to Queenie, her eyes widened with surprise and she exclaimed: "Wolf! — your ears are different. They're pointy!"

I know this sounds daft. Too bad. Life is sometimes exceedingly strange. Queenie had made a study of my ears for twenty years, oohing and aahing about how perfectly shaped they were. Girls like stuff like that: cute ears, straight noses, etc. I don't think she's overly fond of my receding hairline or the fuzz that sprouted on my shoulders but Wolf's ears have been handled, fondled, caressed and annoyingly tickled more or less on a daily basis for two decades, so I take her word for it that their shape suddenly changed. DNA triggers at different stages of life. In puberty, we change dramatically, as I'm sure you remember. At age 45-50, women are released from baby production, change chemistry, and emerge "crowned" with reason and enormous spiritual strength. Think of Ayn Rand at age fifty, totally secure in her knowledge, absolutely certain of her historic achievement in defining the sanction of the victim.

So, I am willing to accept that I've undergone a physical transformation of modest proportions and my ears look more like a Vulcan. That's the least important detail. Indeed, regardless of cause or consequences, my life has been abruptly reorganized. When David came to visit six months ago, I told him the same thing I told people for thirty years, that I was a filmmaker and come hell or high water I was going to direct a 70mm Panavision Hollywood feature. Like Howard Roark, my life was devoted to an artistic career, aiming at a widescreen skyscraper. No more.

Tinsel Town is eclipsed by a dream that gave me pointy ears and a reborn sense of life. No more Mr. Nice Guy — it's time to kick ass and take names.

First on my list is the late Ronald E. Merrill, author of 'The Ideas of Ayn Rand' and the only Objectivist writer I know who had anything sensible to say about Ayn Rand. The rest of this essay is addressed to those who are, like Ron Merrill was, capable of talking sense. What follows is an intellectual ultimatum. It will not be boring or difficult to understand.

Merrill's work was brilliant. If we could describe the entire population of Objectivist scholars as a physical universe, Ron Merrill was nearest to the sun, a self-employed scientist and private entrepreneur — while in some dark frozen asteroid belt beyond Pluto and Goofy, Chris Sciabarra is a Hegelian wanker, Cousin Leonard is lost in space and Nathan thinks the sun shines out of his playful little penis.

Crumbs and stumble bums are unimportant. It's Merrill I'm after. He put a series of questions at the end of The Ideas of Ayn Rand which I will proceed to answer. Let the chips fall where they may.

What is government? Why should rational men submit to it?

Merrill correctly stated that Rand failed to answer these questions, and her lapse sunk the young Objectivists and the Libertarian Party. Government is a mistake. Nothing justifies it. Rational men should not submit to it, if they value their dignity.

Are not libertarian ideas and libertarian policies making progress?

No. My assessments of Cato and Hazlitt are well known. Libertarian vote peddling is mental masturbation. Voting is immoral, because it validates the state. If you describe yourself as a libertarian, I'll wager you have a comfortable lifestyle, a calendar full of social engagements, and a portfolio of paper claims to somebody else's sweat equity. Very brave.

What is to be done?

I answered this in Defacto Anarchy, reprinted by *Laissez Faire City Times* as "Government Is a Quack Faith-Healer." Idle libertarians can help John Galt (1) publicize the declining private sector share of GDP and the growing menace of government; (2) identify religion for the sewer it is; and (3) defend the rights of children by refusing to hand them over to government employees in state and local playschools.

How can a rational person
live in an irrational society?

Take a job at Disney-ABC, if you want to live in an irrational society (or if you believe that an irrational society exists in reality). Folks who ask the above question are trying to duck responsibility for living life on life's terms. As a principle of metaphysics, irrational neighbors are impotent and irrelevant to a rational person's destiny.

How do we live with the rational?

Merrill looked at Galt's Gulch and trembled, didn't want to go there. Fine. If people don't want to grow up, that's their choice. But wishing for a happy ending and peaceful coexistence with Alan Greenspan is more dangerous than burning your bridges to socialism, as you know goddamn well from reading Atlas Shrugged. Stop supporting your destroyers. Quit paying tax and get out. Withdraw the sanction of the victim and join us.

Perhaps most important of all,
how do we live with our families?

Sit your kids down at the kitchen table and explain the facts of life. Mommy and Daddy are not sending them to school, because it's dangerous to their mental health. If your parents and siblings are lost causes, lose them. You have a right to live for your own sake — remember? — therefore, no blood relative has an unearned, intrinsic chokehold on your liberty and happiness.

How will history evaluate Ayn Rand?

It depends on the historian. *The Washington Post* and CNN have no idea who Ayn Rand was. Sciabarra moved nonexistent mountains to prove that she was a confused Hegelian. Ruddy wants to make soap opera sausage of her philosophy. Ayn Rand is dead and buried, my love. All we have left is the courage to lift up our heads, to think for ourselves and go forward, with or without acknowledgment of Dead White Females. If you expect an enemy to honor Rand, there is no point in continuing this discussion.

Much more interesting is: how will history evaluate *you*?

If you think that what I do is easy, you're badly mistaken. I pour three or four days into each article (including this one) — and sometimes it takes every ounce of courage I can muster. "The Decision To Kill" required three weeks of anguish, hating the idea that it was somehow my responsibility to set the facts straight. I don't enjoy the burden of intellectual responsibility. No one does. Phoolan Devi didn't. Pankhurst didn't. Boadicea didn't. Hypatia didn't. Don't know who those martyrs of intellect and justice were? Energize a feminist transporter and beam yourself up a notch.

On the back burner I had a note to myself to write an essay entitled For Want of A Nail. Maybe you already know the fable. For want of a nail the shoe was lost. For want of a shoe the horse was lost. For want of a horse the rider was lost. For want of a rider the message was lost. For want of a message the brigade was lost. For want of a brigade the battle was lost.

This is war. These are your marching orders:

> Get off your ass and get to work. Smash the state.
> Or go down with the rest of the looters and moochers.

Framer of Last Resort

published by Laissez Faire City Times in 2001
reprinted in 'Laissez Faire Law' 2007

I suspect that I am prone to making trouble. And I've decided to make more trouble than usual this year by authoring The Freeman's Constitution. A few months from now, it will take effect as the basis of a new legal system that many of you will reluctantly end up accepting and using as a standard of civil justice and due process among freemen. This article is a 'heads up' on the future of laissez faire law and an invitation to criticize the work of its chief carpenter, while I'm hammering and sawing it.

I know it sounds vain of me to claim Jefferson's role in an era of global speech and wide knowledge. But fess up, neighbor, you haven't done much constitutional thinking, have you? Hate law on principle, huh? That makes me the framer of last resort.

I've written quite a lot about the law for this newspaper [LFC Times]. You'll find articles on property, copyrights, defacto anarchy, and the role of a judiciary under my name in the Writer's Index. *The Good Walk Alone* argued for a private police force, directed by plutocrats and playboys, which is anarcho-capitalism in spirit and tangible fact.

I like liberty so much that I'm willing to admit that the practice of law and profession of justice should be a dinky sideshow in the free market circus. I don't want a state to enforce court orders. Rather, it will be discovered very soon that the public good requires laissez faire law to prevent states from forming in cyberspace.

Too much electronic ink has been devoted to dispute settlement. It is very important to understand that no legal system exists solely for that purpose. The Freeman's Constitution will have little to say on the subject of torts and breach of contract. Private matters are best handled by mediation. Besides which, you have no business doing business with a smooth-talking stranger. The whole point of being a freeman is to conduct your own affairs, win or lose, in an unregulated market. Law cannot absolve you of a folly.

Justice Without Government

What laissez faire law courts can (and must) do is public justice, when the wrong is great and there is nowhere else to turn for closure. Consider a few examples. Assume that a prominent man, an honored patriot of our society is assassinated by culprit or culprits unknown. Who investigates his murder? Who prosecutes? How is guilt or innocence determined? What punishment can we impose for a heinous political act? Leaders exist now at the forefront of our emergent free society, and many more will arise. Only a widely held respect for due process can restrain an epidemic of private vengence, if there is bloodshed.

It is no answer to say that we should rely on extant nation states to prosecute crime or adjudicate real property rights. By summoning the devil of government, you accept its claim of tyrannical privilege and everything that goes with it: SSI numbers, citizenship and taxes. The last place I would report a crime is at a police station. Cops enjoy detaining and interrogating freemen, and they routinely share information with the FBI and IRS. We need a laissez faire agency of law and order, entirely independent of sovereign nation states, because governments seek above all else to suppress tax evasion and undocumented travel. Unless you plan to open your castle to the IRS, DEA, U.S. Customs and an infinity of bureaucrats as the price of admission to public justice, at some point in the future a horrifying crime in our lawless community will inspire you to concede that outlaws, too, need recourse to an impartial tribunal of our kind.

Another example: a spectacular banking fraud or embezzlement suddenly wipes out hundreds of accountholders. Each accountholder was wronged, and each can sue. But some wrongs damage the public good — especially if an innocent man or group is falsely accused of misconduct.

The law establishes limits of liability, enforceability of contracts, and the obligation of a fiduciary. Due process exonerates the falsely accused, as well as those who may be guilty but against whom no provable case can be made.

Another example: people die of old age. You cannot forever manage your own affairs, and laissez faire courts are needed to probate the disposition of your estate. If you die or declare yourself bankrupt, your remaining assets should be properly distributed to your creditors, according to a complex hierarchy of contract and property law. Your heirs must be discharged and held harmless.

Lastly, perhaps most importantly, the imperative of national security will never recede. A laissez faire community, however small, is a nation of bandits and scofflaws, each of our names destined to appear on a list somewhere as suspected criminals, perhaps revolutionaries. Every day of a freeman's life involves breaking some nation state's regulations and edicts. This compels freemen to adopt and observe a rigorous system of disguises and financial defenses, including the use of aliases. A mole in our midst can do enormous damage to the community, and so, we logically support the activities, if any, of our Intelligence and Security agencies, if such groups exist. We need a laissez faire constitution to stop the 'good guys' from falsely accusing and peremptorily punishing innocent people. It has happened before. It will happen again. The most urgent responsibility of a laissez faire judiciary is to propagate the rule of law as a counterweight to secret use of explusion and surveillance by Executive Order. It feels foolish to pretend that there is no Executive Branch or administrative agency in our community, no central bank, no stock exchange, etc, but I'm willing to do so, for national security reasons. What I am not willing to do is to cede arbitrary power to a defacto state, policed by anonymous spooks. If the Executive wants to conduct a digital search or seizure, make them apply for a court order. Laissez faire judges, upholding the Freeman's Constitution, are sworn to defend innocent liberty and privacy, unless there is probable cause to investigate a crime. Treason is a crime. So is espionage.

Laissez Faire Courts

Omitting national security problems, I suppose critics will assume that it is but a foolish man's fantasy that laissez faire courts will spring into existence. This is a misunderstanding of my position. Laissez faire courts will not spring into existence because Wolf DeVoon said so, but because laissez faire lawyers will surely need them. It is only a matter of time, and I have been informed that time is short. LESE and DMT are about to roll out — a modern equivalent of Concord and Lexington, 'A Shot Heard Round the World.'

I respect very sincerely the prejudice of my fellow freemen, who are angrily contemptuous of all lawyers and law. No doubt they believe themselves able to compose their own contracts and corporate charters, unaided by advice of legal counsel. Not everyone is equally competent. Many need representation, especially in the event of a dispute. All of us need recourse to an impartial tribunal when shit comes to holler and tests our community's institutions. It is good that no one wants government. But the law is not government.

Law is a profession, like medicine or engineering, and freemen need objective public justice if they wish to enjoy their liberty and privacy. To some, it is a painful truth that science is not arbitrary supposition. To others it's intolerable to be legally answerable to a summons and called into court, either as a witness or defendant. The rule of law is not fun. It is a difficult duty that no one much enjoys, not even when you prevail over an adversary in court.

But the alternative of lawlessness is worse than due process, which is why I am certain that most freemen will join me, sooner or later. To participate in the Constitutional Convention, please email your comments or criticism as each constitutional article is posted. Letters from trusted colleagues and thoughtful persons will be published as a matter of historical record. One of the principal failings of the Federal Convention of 1787 was the fact that its debates were kept secret from the public until long after voters ratified a sweeping charter of power, which only a minority of delegates supported.

Happily, the Convention of 2001 has fewer framers (just one, me). There is no delegation of slave owners and clerics to placate. The final result will be a work of logic, rather than political compromise. I wholeheartedly urge you to post your dissent, if any, and let a candid world choose whether your view of law or mine best describes the public good.

You might be pleasantly surprised by the Freeman's Constitution. Unlike the fundamental laws of nation states, my work began with an axiom of political principle, that justice is the armed defense of innocent liberty.

The Freeman's Constitution

Final draft, August 19, 2001

"Justice is the armed defense of innocent liberty."

The purposes and limitations of a first principle are: (1) to establish the context and scope of discussion; (2) to affirm the existence of a fundamental truth pertaining to the topic generally; and (3) to define that truth, employing the least ambiguous and most cognitively fruitful concepts that are logically germane to the definition. Men and women have reasoned about law for centuries. Familiar terms, the relations of which are obvious in the structure of a predicate, compel any adversary to concede or to contradict squarely, because a first principle necessarily addresses a fundamental question. The most fundamental issue in law is justice — not electoral processes or delegated powers, but the right to public justice.

Definitions of justice proffered by others have been lengthy, covering hundreds of pages, intertwining dozens of terms. However, logic is an exact science. Verbosity indicates lack of understanding or deliberate obfuscation. That's why my definition of justice is succinct. A complete theory of justice is presented in one proposition, consisting of one object, one action, and two qualifiers: Justice = armed defense of innocent liberty. The qualifiers are necessary for precision. Verbal defense of liberty isn't justice. It must be armed defense. Not all liberty, just innocent liberty (e.g., the liberty of women and children, who are often unable to defend themselves).

My definition does not refer to or imply any ethical principle. The philosophy of law is a separate branch of science, independent of ethics. Moral inquiry pertains specifically to the interests, powers, and dilemmas of an individual, epitomized by the question: "What shall I do?" Legal philosophy addresses impersonal administration of public justice, litigation among parties in dispute, the combined might of a community, and custodial guardianship of certain individuals who are unable or legally prohibited to conduct their own affairs.

> **"No freeman shall be arrested or imprisoned or disseized or outlawed or exiled or in any way victimized, except by the lawful judgement of his peers and by the law of the land." (Magna Carta, 1215 A.D.)**

Very early in the history of Anglo-American law it was asserted that a freeman was at liberty to conduct his own affairs, unless restrained by due process of law (i.e., a constitution). The notion of "innocent liberty" is easily discerned in this ancient statement of political right. Freemen were at liberty, presumed innocent unless proved guilty of violating the law, which applied equally to all freemen. I do not suggest that this provision of Magna Carta should be construed as an obligatory legal or constitutional precedent. Rather, I cite it to suggest that my theory of justice is not at odds with historical understanding of civil liberty and the rule of law.

The essential function of law is to distinguish between innocence and guilt, truth and falsehood, political right and wrong.

> **"The power exerted by a legal regime consists less in the force that it can bring to bear against violators of its rules than in its capacity to persuade people that the world described in its images and categories is the only attainable world in which a sane person would want to live." (Robert Gordon)**

Every Fourth of July, my fellow countrymen celebrate the mistaken notion that the United States was conceived in liberty. This reveals how little our constitutional history is studied. The U.S. Constitution was not conceived at all — it was a bastard product of compromise and contentious debate, winning ratification by a slim margin among the 20 percent of colonial population who were eligible to vote for assemblies of state politicians who narrowly approved it: Pennsylvania 46-23, Virginia 89-79, New York 30-27. The U.S. Constitution did not provide any definition of justice.

I accept that many previous generations endorsed the American Federal establishment by acquiescence, understanding only that their national government was a small, weak, often laughable cesspool of graft, which prior to 1860 had no control over private life and freedom of contract. There was no Federal income tax, no regulation of domestic commerce, and minimal entanglement in foreign affairs. Only in the 20th century did the U.S. begin in earnest to exert intrusive, dictatorial control of every citizen's private life and civil liberty. Today, all business owners are compelled to serve as tax collectors (income tax withholding, Social Security, and Medicare). Global income is taxed, all investment gains are taxed, and an immense code of rules govern the operation of banking. The result is a nation of political sheep, following the most conservative in our midst. It is a tragedy of unequalled horror, that the meek are led routinely by dangerous and devious charismatics. The only way to rectify this unfolding political disaster is to articulate an alternative legal system, based on a simple proposition that enshrines liberty as the cornerstone of justice.

The Freeman's Constitution does not claim sovereignty in a geographic area, but rather the world at large, affirming that you have an inalienable constitutional right to innocent liberty which no state may lawfully abridge. This bedrock principle of justice is not reiterated in the detailed provisions which follow. Instead, it is the legal standard by which *all* of the provisions of The Freeman's Constitution must be interpreted and measured in practice.

ARTICLE I
THE RIGHT TO PETITION

Any natural person who is not in contempt may petition the courts and enjoy the full protection of due process of law, including appellate review and petition for writ of certiorari in the Supreme Court as a matter of natural right. A natural person who is unable or declines to personally appear may appoint an attorney of his own choosing to appear on his behalf. Attorneys shall be admitted to the practice of law upon appointment by any client, but may be publically censured or disbarred for gross incompetence or misconduct. In the interests of justice, courts may appoint competent counsel to assist or represent any natural person who is indigent, or deemed to be in contempt of court, or insane, or mentally incompetent, or deceased, or a minor under 16 years of age. Associations, partnerships, corporations, trusts, and sovereign states may sue or be sued, provided that any attorney-in-fact who represents a fictional legal person in court shall certify that all of the representatives, officers, agents, and fiduciaries of such person will obey all lawful orders that the court may issue. If suit is brought against a fictional legal person, any and all of its representatives, officers, agents, and fiduciaries may be summoned to appear. Willful and repeated failure to appear when summoned may be deemed an admission of contempt, punishable by up to five years in exile and outlaw, during which persons ruled in contempt shall enjoy no standing to sue, no right to due process, and no right to public justice.

COMMENTS ON ARTICLE I

To be outlawed for contempt is a heavy punishment. Stripped of the protection of law, an outlaw has no right to life or liberty, innocent or otherwise. His bankers can empty an outlawed account, his friends and associates are forced to think twice about entering into or continuing to honor what are now illegal, unenforceable agreements with an outlaw, and his personal safety is put in jeopardy, since an outlaw may be detained or harmed by any law abiding person with impunity. There is no greater punishment that public justice allows, than a sentence of outlaw. For this reason, the courts of first instance are not permitted to impose such a punishment without appointing counsel to represent the person accused of contempt, for the purpose of appeal. The presumption of innocence is integral to due process, and the punishment for contempt amounts to a bill of attainder. Appellate judges are not likely to affirm a sentence of exile and outlaw, unless the evidence of contempt is overwhelming and the entire record of the trial court case shows that the accused fled prosecution for felony and the complainant had sufficient evidence and sworn testimony to obtain a grand jury indictment. **WD, 8/3/01**

ARTICLE II
THE POWER TO APPOINT AND REMOVE JUDGES

Five or more attorneys, acting on behalf of ten or more natural persons, may convene a court of first instance by electing one of their number to serve as a law judge. Any natural person may serve as a law judge, unless debarred for cause and forbidden to practice law by order of the Supreme Court or any inferior appellate court established by the Supreme Court. A law judge of first instance and his clerk shall be remunerated by equal contributions levied upon and serve at the pleasure of a majority of attorneys admitted to practice law in that court. To make these provisions effective, a majority of the first twenty signatories to this Constitution shall assemble or correspond for the purpose of nominating one or more members of the first

Supreme Court, whose appointment shall become effective when confirmed by the Supervisors or Governors or such other style of Representative Body of Founders who are empowered by Laissez Faire City to review matters pertaining to its governance and redress of grievances. The Chief Justice and additional Associate Justices shall be nominated by the Chief Executive of Laissez Faire City, all such appointments becoming effective if confirmed by a majority ballot of sitting law judges of first instance. Justices of the Supreme Court and inferior appellate judges shall serve during good behavior or until voluntary retirement and may not be removed, unless impeached by the City's Representative Body of Founders and convicted of misconduct by a majority ballot of law judges of first instance.

COMMENTS ON ARTICLE II

No official or Founder of Laissez Faire City advised or consented to promulgation of this Article. No official or Founder of Laissez Faire City should be construed to have, now or at any time in the future, a favorable opinion of this constitution or any intent to execute the powers of appointment and removal conferred by this Article. That said, it is equally true that Laissez Faire City is addressed and referenced above as a defacto nation in need of a constitutional judiciary and due process of law, which has occupied my thoughts for two consecutive years. **WD, 8/3/01**

Majority rule is seldom good, but there is little other choice with respect to public officeholders (such as law judges). The defunct Articles of Confederation, which governed the United States during its infancy as a republic, required the unanimous consent of all 13 states to enact or enforce law and promptly collapsed as a constitutional entity, because any individual state could withhold its consent and frustrate the manifest public good. That's why the Federal Convention was held, as an emergency conference of "wise men" to negotiate a majority-based balance of power among Large States and Small States, Free States and Slave States. The only thing they agreed on was a statist paradigm, reflecting the widely held Christian view that God had ordained the Americans to seize "the separate and equal station" of sovereignty that monarchies claimed. Today, we are in a vastly different context. The Freeman's Constitution does not ordain or establish a state. Rather, it is the organizational law of the laissez faire bar. It gives practicing lawyers the right to convene and the duty to pay for courts of first instance, and judges must command the confidence of a majority of their professional colleagues to remain on the bench. **WD, 8/4/01**

In a laissez faire community of any kind, physical or digital, the rule of law arises from and requires all of the following: a constitutional right to practice legal representation on behalf of others; the right of practicing lawyers to associate for the purpose of selecting judges who, on appointment to the bench, are barred from private legal practice; and the right of any person or organized group to obey and execute lawful orders that may be issued from time to time by the courts so created. The jursidiction of laissez faire constitutional law and the courts which duly interpret and uphold such principles exists globally and perpetually as a matter of right. Laissez faire constitutional law flows from a single proposition, which is that no one may legally judge his own cause of action or act to penalize another without fair public trial and impartial due process of law. Laissez faire law is discovered and demonstrated in the process of litigation and trial. It cannot be legislated, codified, or imposed by a "lawgiver." **WD, Opinion of Counsel, 1/12/00**

ARTICLE III
VENUES AND CAUSES OF ACTION

The common law right to trial by a jury of one's peers, drawn at random from the full list of living natural persons signatory to this

Constitution, shall be limited in family law cases to a jury of women. In all except felony cases, trial by jury may be waived by unanimous, informed consent of all parties to the proceeding. Complaints of misdemeanor or felony shall be heard in a trial court that is licensed by the Supreme Court to conduct police proceedings. Each of the parties to a criminal case must be represented by a criminal barrister, a distinction to be awarded according to the wisdom of the Laissez Faire Bar Association.

Other courts of first instance may hear and adjudicate cases and controversies according to the specialty of practice selected by a majority of the court's attorneys, or hold a general civil session if subscribed by more than twenty attorneys. All constitutional questions must originate in a lower court, unless one or more parties named in a petition is a sovereign state, in which case the Supreme Court shall have original jurisdiction.

From time to time, the Supreme Court may create, regulate, fund, and appoint judges to appellate courts, whose jurisdiction over courts of first instance shall be apportioned randomly by date of appeal and without regard to legal specialty. All pleadings shall be styled "In defense of innocent liberty," and all plaintiffs shall allege that the peti-tioner's enjoyment of life, liberty, or settled claim to property was or will be wrongly impaired or taken without due process of law.

COMMENTS ON ARTICLE III

Associations, partnerships, corporations, trusts, states, and other fictional legal persons have no intrinsic right to life or liberty. The fundamental legal character of all such entities is that of shared or managed property, title to which is in dispute. Fictional legal persons cannot prosecute crime, other than misdemeanor trespass or burglary. Laissez faire law does not recognize the "sovereign power" of a state to levy taxes, issue passports, coin money, or regulate banking or commerce. **WD, 8/6/01**

ARTICLE IV
THE POLICE POWER

The right to keep and bear arms and to use reasonable force in defense of one's life and innocent liberty, or the life and liberty of another, describes the police power generally. Every person signatory to this Constitution is lawfully empowered to arrest and detain a perpetrator or willing accessory apprehended during the commission of a crime. From time to time, the Supreme Court may establish, regulate, fund, and appoint officers to an investigative agency or custodial facilities for the humane detention of persons accused of felony, and in all cases detainees must appear before a criminal magistrate within 24 hours of arrest. No accused person shall be bound over for trial unless there is actionable evidence of crime and credible testimony to establish probable cause for complaint. All felony prosecutions shall be conducted on behalf of a living natural person whose enjoyment of life, liberty, or settled claim to property are alleged to have been impaired. In cases of public nuisance or acts injurious to a communications network, database, bank or exchange, courts may order natural or fictional persons to cease and desist. Willful and repeated failure to obey such an order may be deemed an admission of contempt. There is no personal right to exact vengeance or to obstruct justice and due process of law. Any person convicted of willfully and wrongfully invoking the police power may be punished by life exile and outlaw.

COMMENTS ON ARTICLE IV

The most serious crime of all is abuse of the police power, and the Constitution provides the sternest possible punishment (basically, the death penalty) for willfully and wrongfully denying another person's legal presumption of innocence and right to due process. Note also that in homicide cases, prosecution made is on behalf of a survivor – a grieving spouse, dependent child, or business associate. "The earth belongs in usufruct to the living." (Jefferson) **WD, 8/6/01**

ARTICLE V
THE RIGHT TO REVOLUTION

When otherwise law abiding and peaceful freemen are imperiled as a class by force of arms, or arrest and imprisonment, or conscription, or surveillance, or involuntary taxation levied by a state or legislature in denial and derogation of innocent liberty, such acts of terrorism and oppression shall be interpreted as a campaign of war against humanity, and every natural person or group acting in concert possesses the legal right and duty to throw off such tyranny and to resist its evil by prudent and vigorous self-defense, including but not limited to flight, armed rebellion, sabotage, and use of disguise to avoid capture. No man shall be prosecuted for crime or sued for damages in respect of his service in a revolutionary war, except in cases where wanton bloodshed or private vengeance or impairment of individual liberty or property was willfully perpetrated by a person or conspiracy to thwart civil due process of law.

COMMENTS ON ARTICLE V

A state of revolutionary war exists at the time of this writing and shall likely continue during the indefinite future, until the United States of America ceases to assert its "sovereign power" over free men and women, whose right to innocent liberty admits of no limitation by legislatures, territorial states, or previous condition of citizenship.

Defects in The Freeman's Constitution

written in 2002 and refused publication by LFC
published in 'Laissez Faire Law' 2007

I won't pretend to be an opponent of The Freeman's Constitution, but
I am painfully aware that it has multiple and woeful defects. Many
are political conundrums unsolvable by law as such.

The lengthy Preamble on justice has a gigantic hole in the middle of
its logic, which my friend Thomas E. Ruppenthal rightly objected to
six months ago, while we were filming *Inside Wolf DeVoon*. I merrily
defined justice as the armed defense of innocent liberty, and Tom
huffed: "Who's holding the arms?"

In truth, I don't know. It probably won't be laissez faire law courts, if
they are governed according to Articles II-IV. There is no source of
funding provided for the Supreme Court or for law enforcement.
Taxation is nixed by Article V as a source of revenue. Laissez faire
lawyers and judges certainly aren't going to form themselves into a
police squad. As the cynical Scottish phrase explains it, 'Good talkers
are nae good doers.' Law clients often consider themselves fortunate
if an attorney answers the telephone without charging them $125 an
hour to say hello. The entire mechanism of public justice is an
expensive, largely formal ritual of paperwork and seemingly
interminable delay, until a court order is executed by someone else --
typically, by one of the parties in a case, who waited an eternity to get
the legal okey-doke to do something they wanted to do and could
have done a lot quicker. I honestly don't know anyone who enjoys
lawful due process. I certainly don't, and I never did.

The point of suffering through a courtroom drama is to honor James
Madison's epigram of fairness: that no man should be allowed to
judge his own cause. That's why lawyers, judges and juries make
sense, not only in the specific situation of creating and advancing a

new nation of digital freemen, but also in the historical sense that every society in the past faced the same issue and paid similar heed to a tribunal of reasoned inquiry, hoping to supplant unequal, reckless private combat with impartial due process.

In distant and primitive eons, 'law courts' were an ad hoc council of elders around the campfire, or a hearing before the village chieftain. During the Christian Era, bishops decided cases involving lesser mortals (obviously, an embarrassingly dark passage for the rule of law). Ignoring the British and American common law tradition, where adversarial due process evolved into a bulwark of civil liberty, elsewhere in the 20th century, Imperial Japan, Nazi Germany, Soviet Russia, Red China, and every tinpot dictator from Bolivia to Botswana made a gesture of some sort to due process and claimed that their kangaroo courts were 'impartial.' Why? — because dictators in particular and men in general **never** admit to evil. The bloodiest villains always cling to the idea that they're right and just; that their actions, however cruel and horrible, are sanctified by some sort of 'mission' or moral code.

Some of my critics have asserted that the best law is no law, pleading a bald contradiction in terms, as if acquittal was their birthright, a perfect haven of immunity, guarded by an impassable moat. Men are incapable of confessing openly that they want to escape justice. Friend or enemy of due process, we declare with one voice that our conduct is fair and honorable, with malice toward none. The claim is usually false. In simple, 18th century language: Men are not angels. Our protestations of innocence and truth are frequently exaggerated and unwarranted. That's why we need courts of justice, with compulsory production of evidence, crossexamination, and felony penalties for perjury. Men lie. We also remember wrongly, forget, etc. Evildoers should not be allowed to judge their own innocence. Nor is it sane or wise to treat accusation as proof, condemning someone without fair trial of fact.

The need for justice overlays so closely the enterprise of human life that no man can leave the subject unattended for very long. Every article published in this newspaper [Laissez Faire City Times] asks us to consider some grievance involving, at bottom, the want of justice, because men do wrong and lie about it afterwards.

So, I repeat my earlier admission: The Freeman's Constitution is silent on the question of enforcement. Paperwork cannot enforce the decisions rendered by judges or juries. Someone else will have to establish an Executive Branch and, by the grace of right reason, diligently subordinate its police power to the ponderously complicated rule of law.

For instance, it has been announced that MailVault will not transmit child pornography. Good policy. However, it fertilizes a bunch of legal thistles: How do we define 'child pornography'? If email messages facilitate postal or courier delivery of the banned stuff, is that banned, too? How will anybody detect wrongful use of encrypted messages? Assuming detection, what penalty will be levied? —and by whom? Laissez faire law courts can help settle these questions (and hopefully safeguard the rights of those mistakenly or maliciously accused of porno trade), but finally, it's up to the proprietors of MailVault to obey and execute a court order.

The law is mostly voluntary, folks. I acknowledged this openly and emphatically in my essay 'Government Is A Quack Faith-Healer'. If there is to be law and order, you yourselves will be the police of it. *The Good Walk Alone* was a fair portrait of our enlightened future — two dozen cops for a self-governing city of 40,000 — relying on the civic strength of a free society to mostly police itself, which means: settling your disputes by seeking legal guidance voluntarily from an unarmed judiciary, whose chief weapon is reason.

Why then provide a constitutional judiciary at all? Why not an arbitration service or legal think tank? — or maybe several competing courts since none of them can do a damn thing about enforcement? Again, the Freeman's Constitution is unhelpfully mute on these alternatives, blowing them off with its assertion of global and perpetual jurisdiction, as if nothing else was worth discussing.

Obviously, alternatives should be given urgent consideration. Arbitration is a flourishing component of modern U.S. practice and must be implemented in our digital community as speedily as possible. A legal think tank is a great idea. We certainly need one. And in practical reality, we are surrounded by competing courts (U.S. and Costa Rican in particular). Undoubtedly our lawyers will be required to understand and cope with three totally different legal systems, plus arbitration. Even in my own ears, it sounds rather ridiculous that laissez faire law will someday prevail as the sole and supreme institution of public justice.

Yet, that's what revolution presupposes — that deep, lasting political change is possible and that we can create new institutions, in particular a public legal system without a state, comprised of private law courts whose organization is left mainly in the hands of practicing lawyers.

I know that doesn't sound fair, because it treats law as the privileged domain of those skilled in the art. But if you banned the practice of medicine because doctors dominated its science, I don't think you'd be very pleased with the result. Yes, it's possible to obtain a form of rough justice conducted by laymen, just as you can nurse a head cold with home remedies — but medicine is far more than tongue depressors and aspirin. Amateurs can neither x-ray nor set a fractured pelvis. The law is vastly complicated because the nature of humanity is complex, such that it requires a dozen specialties of legal practice: corporate, commercial, criminal, family, probate, torts, maritime, equity, bankruptcy, trial, constitutional, and political (i.e., national security and legislative matters). My specialty is human rights and constitutional law. I don't know beans about maritime or probate, both of which have huge bodies of case law, full of closely reasoned debates about hundreds of questions that I really don't want to tangle with.

The Freeman's Constitution is a blank page in many respects, because it calls on freedom loving lawyers, young and old, to come forward and build a new practice, as a matter of professional duty. I have no clue what might become, say, the laissez faire law of marriage, divorce, and child custody. What little I established is a fundamental constitutional principle, that every natural person (Mom, Dad, and each of the kids) has the right to petition the courts on their own behalf or to appoint an attorney to represent them. Family law courts will be organized mainly by divorce lawyers and the clients who engage their services. Petitioners always have more power than lawyers, because they drive the whole thing with legal fees and particular (sometimes quite bizarre) causes, with very little pre-ordained constitutional guidance. The basic idea of The Freeman's Constitution is that it empowers many litigants to argue and help adjudicate case law. That's why I commend to your conscience a social compact with a lot of blanks to be filled in, much of its potential justice inert and unknown, unless you and your attorney endeavor to define it.

However, this is not to say that the Constitution is structureless or lacking in substantive content. Article IV is an achievement of historic merit, linking the right to bear arms and the police power. Article V is a declaration of political independence from all previous notions of sovereignty.

I know that some of you wish to use the term 'sovereign individual,' to denote your liberation from the old nostrums of citizenship. I do not demur, except to warn that liberty is not a personal attribute that dies when you die. Only impartial public justice spans many lifetimes and liberties of equally free persons engaged in myriad controversies, of which yours may be the least important, if you seldom sue anyone and commit no crime. The law labors longest and most diligently on behalf of those who rightly seek its protection from those who wrongly think themselves above it.

It is only in the context of revolution that The Freeman's Constitution makes real sense, because it ordains and establishes a higher legal authority than the United States of America (or any other territorial state). Perhaps in 'libertopia' someday, the practice of law will wither away, no longer needed. But for now and the foreseeable future, I remain in awe of a political truth equally certain to your abhorance of 'unnecessary' legal expense:

> *As we look back over the long story of the nations, we must see that their glory has been founded upon the spirit of resistance to tyranny and injustice, especially when those evils seemed to be backed by heavier force. Since the dawn of the Christian era, a certain way of life has slowly been shaping itself among the Western peoples, and certain standards of conduct and government have come to be esteemed. After many miseries and prolonged confusion, there arose into the broad light of day the conception of the right of the individual; his right to be consulted in the government of his country; his right to invoke the law even against the State itself. Independent courts of justice were created to affirm and enforce this hard-won custom. Thus was assured throughout the English speaking world, and in France by the stern lessons of the Revolution, what Kipling called "Leave to live by no man's leave underneath the law." Now in this resides all that makes existence precious to man and all that confers honor and health upon the state.*
>
> (Winston Churchill, October 16, 1938)

I realize that The Freeman's Constitution could be twisted and misinterpreted into the shape of a state. It is an admitted weakness, that its future is utterly dependent upon the character and wisdom of the laissez faire bar. As clients and paying customers, lay freemen wield the market power of democracy, expressed in who they appoint as attorneys. Appoint none and our infant nation will never grow straight and tall, as Dora would say: "With a backbone instead of a wishbone." Ultimately, it is the moral backbone of the many, by their appointment of legal representatives to courts of justice and by separate legislation to govern a powerful Executive, that will determine the surety and stability of our economic infrastructure.

We The People must voluntarily ratify the Freeman's Constitution and pledge to enforce it with every talon and claw. Bankers, investors, and ordinary folks around the world are waiting for us to pick up the sword of justice.

Freemen won't subdue tyranny, or make much of a profit, unless the fiduciary duty of laissez faire bankers is defined and objectively policed with unbiased justice in defense of private title to property.

I know it seems paradoxical: public due process is conducted in open court; how can anything remain private, much less anonymous? Quite simple. Cases are A vs B, and court orders can be issued on a need to know basis. The only facts that should be published in a newspaper of record are: appellate decisions, declarations of bankruptcy, class actions, and the identity of persons convicted of felony.

If a member of the public wishes to attend a hearing or trial court proceeding, they can log on to a filtered version of the official transcript that anonymizes the identity of the parties before the bar, but which names all the lawyers and judges, whose colloquies and instructions are attributed, so that bad lawyers can be disbarred and bad judges removed. My professional colleagues are already accustomed to walking on thin political ice in the glare of hostile scrutiny, every legal word, thought, and deed documented in public records.

National

Defense

How stupid are we?

In 1996, a wealthy Saudi cleric issued a fatwā calling for American soldiers to leave Saudi Arabia. In a second fatwā issued in 1998, he repeated the condemnation of American troops stationed in Saudi Arabia: "For over seven years the United States has been occupying the lands of Islam in the holiest of places, the Arabian Peninsula."

A few days after the 9/11 WTC and Pentagon attacks, the FBI identified all 19 hijackers. Fifteen of the men were from Saudi Arabia. So, why didn't we bomb Saudi Arabia? The 9/11 attack was planned and led by an Egyptian. Why didn't we bomb Egypt?

Capturing or killing the wealthy Saudi cleric, Osama bin Laden, had been a national security objective of the U.S. government since 1998. Bill Clinton directed the CIA to apprehend bin Laden and bring him to the U.S. to stand trial, or if taking him alive was too difficult, then deadly force was authorized. In August 1998, the U.S. Navy fired 66 cruise missiles at bin Laden's camp in Afghanistan, narrowly missing him by a few hours. In 2000, CIA operatives fired an RPG at a convoy of vehicles in which bin Laden was traveling, hitting one of the cars, but not the one in which bin Laden was riding. In other words we attacked Osama bin Ladin repeatedly, long before September 11, 2001 — and then blamed *him* for attacking us?

Saddam Hussein had absolutely nothing to do with 9/11. So, why did we invade and occupy Iraq at a cost of $2 trillion and 4,400 dead? — not counting 1.8 million refugees and 100,000 Iraqi dead. In 2005, a Pentagon study found that one in four U.S. troops who survived the Iraq War came home with health problems that required medical or mental health treatment, over 79,000 casualties. U.S. officials accused Saddam of harboring and supporting al-Qaeda, but no evidence of a connection was ever discovered. They also claimed that Saddam had WMD — none were found.

Vietnam

excerpt from 'Flag, Faith, and Family Values'
published by Free Liberal magazine, 2005

Vietnam was a brutal "asymmetrical" war that few U.S. conscripts could have been proud to have prosecuted. Two million Vietnamese were killed; 4.5 million wounded; 6,500,000 women, children and elderly made homeless refugees.

To put this in perspective, imagine that China someday decides to attack the United States and deploys its U.S. espionage network to bollix our computer addicted chain of command so badly that co-ordinated homeland defense is impossible. Further suppose that a wave of Chinese nukes incinerate 30 million U.S. civilians and poisons half of our food supply. That's basically what we did to Vietnam. Ten percent of the Vietnamese population were killed and thousands of square miles of forest and river were poisoned with Agent Orange.

Incredibly, destruction and carnage amounting to genocide were justified by **selfless altruism.**

"An important part of the reason we marched into Vietnam with eyes fixed was liberalism's irrepressible need to be helpful to those less fortunate. But the decency of the impulse cannot hide the bloody eagerness to kill in the name of virtue. In 1981, James C. Thomson, a member of the National Security Council under President Johnson, finally concluded that our Vietnamese intervention had been motivated by a national missionary impulse, a 'need to do good to others.' In a phrase that cannot be improved, he and others called this 'sentimental imperialism.' The purity of intention and the horror of result are unfortunately the liberals' continuing burden...

"Conservatives shared with liberals the conviction that America could act, and in Vietnam did act, with absolute altruism, as they believed only America could. Thinking of this war, President Nixon declared that 'never in history have men fought for less selfish motives — not for conquest, not for glory, but only for the right of a people far away to choose the kind of government they want.' " (Loren Baritz, Backfire)

For 30 years, enduring the hell of occupation and B-52 bombardment, what the Vietnamese wanted was government by anyone except the U.S. Army and a string of lunatic Saigon dictators who Americans lavished with luxuries and unchecked power.

"Diem legalized his brutality by creating special military courts to try [approximately 40,000] political opponents and to pass sentences of death in no more than three days... A reluctant Vice-President Johnson was sent to review conditions in South Vietnam. While abroad he informed the world that Diem was the 'Winston Churchill of Southeast Asia.' When a reporter asked LBJ if he meant what he had said, he answered: 'Shit, Diem's the only boy we got out there!'...

"July 1965 was when President Johnson lost control of the war in Vietnam and America. It was then that he made the decision to raise the level of killing and committed America to what the most thoughtful military men had consistently warned about: a land war in Asia...

"A few months earlier there had been another change of political leadership in South Vietnam. [Coup leader and new prime minister] Ky liked to dress in black or bright yellow silk fatigues decorated with a vivid scarf, and toted an ivory-handled pistol. He admired Adolph Hitler more than any other Western statesman. He worked hard to earn a reputation as a gambler, boozer, and womanizer. Gen. Westmoreland liked Ky because 'he was a man of action, a swashbuckler'." (Baritz, ibid.)

What good is the state?

an excerpt from 'Defacto Anarchy' written in 1998
published and reprinted many times

No public work was raised without delay, confusion, cost overrun, graft, or outright disaster as a final consequence. Every morning the state mangles reason and justice to perform simple tasks that private actors (a) would not undertake because the project is stupid; or (b) could do faster, cheaper, and better than government; or (c) are required to do anyway, since the state has no competence except that which is supplied by private contractors. All the U.S. politicians and bureaucrats combined could not repair a flush toilet.

I become bored with discussing the state's incompetence, so obvious a fact. The worst toxic waste sites are government property. The Soviet Union wrought environmental catastrophe, because wanton misery and economic folly are proportionate to the size of government. They never learn, never fail to make stupid decisions. This week Boris Yeltsin spent $3.5 billion of IMF cash trying (and failing) to defend the rouble, precisely reproducing Black Wednesday, when Britain emptied her purse trying (and failing) to defend the ERM.

"Bad protection drives out good," Alan Greenspan used to say. If the peace and prosperity of the world rests on Bill Clinton's shoulders, how does the Commander-In-Chief have time to masturbate in the Oval Office during office hours? Answer: *Peace and prosperity don't.* Politicians have nothing of consequence to do, say, or decide. They are physiocratic wind-up toys, floating in a bubblebath of lukewarm hysteria, reciting platitudes written by schoolboys. We prosper to the extent that government does nothing. Clinton feels our pain, didn't inhale, whimpers for forgiveness. If there is any justification for this carnival of hot air, it must be discerned from an abstraction, because none of the empirical data suggest any tangible benefit produced by these sterile public employments.

"Supposedly, there exist important services, such as national defense, which benefit people whether they pay for them or not. The result is that selfish agents refuse to contribute, leading to disaster. The only way to solve this problem is to coerce the beneficiaries to raise the funds to supply the needed good. In order for this coercion to work, it needs to be monopolized by a single agency, the state. Public goods arguments have been made not only for national defense, but for police, roads, education, R&D, scientific research, and many other goods and services. The essential definitional feature of public goods is 'non-excludability'; because the benefits cannot be limited to contributors, there is no incentive to contribute." (Bryan Caplan, Anarchy FAQ)

How this justifies the Vietnam War or the defense of Kuwait is impossible to guess. So, let's suppose that it's 1939 and our national security problem is Adolph Hitler. Selfish plutocrats are weary of throwing good U.S. savings after bad, rescuing England. Jewish Americans raise funds to help their kinfolk in Poland, and German-Americans parade through Wisconsin waving swastikas. These are historical facts. It is undeniably true that, at any moment in history, the community will be divided into rival interest groups, each demanding that all the others contribute to some "public good." I am not an infantile individualist, demanding the right to be let alone by my neighbors or by whichever dominant faction has control of the elephantine mousetrap of state. Nor is David Friedman's example of housetrailers in France a solution. We do not live in housetrailers. Our lives and fortunes are deeply rooted in geographical community. Try building a factory or a nuclear power station on a housetrailer! Even in some micro-agrarian society, where the population is geographically dispersed and scatters farther into the hills at the first whiff of trouble, like the peasants of Cosovo, the penalty for isolation is deprivation, and ultimately you run out of room to run. Kropotkin's "sensible dictates of tribal conscience" are a joke, when the problem is a ruthless neighbor like Adolph Hitler mobilizing twenty Panzer divisions with absolute air supremacy.

The solution here is at ground zero, the foundation of society. If the American government had been disbanded in 1910 (to pick a date when it might have been historically feasible) the problem of Adolph Hitler would never have arisen. The mass suicide of World War I would have ended without Wilson's mismanagement. There would have been no Great Depression to bankrupt postwar Europe. The American society of 1933, sans Franklin Roosevelt, would have been free of Keynesian doctrine, trading in hard currency and guided by a consortium of wealthy private bankers and industrialists — a vastly different regime than Kropotkin's "tribal conscience."

American military adventures in Europe and Asia have always been pointless and unprofitable, from a strictly commercial perspective. War is an irrational waste of resources that no business would dare undertake. Consequently, the capitalist policy of national defense is to: (a) maximize industrial output; (b) maintain a strategic intelligence network; and (c) when necessary, call upon the whole community for men and munitions to meet any clear and present danger, providing capital and moral support to those who volunteer to fight.

If this seems preposterously simple, then you have not read the history of the American Revolution. Most people are not mercenaries; they will not fight for money alone, unless they perceive that their communities and their loved ones are in real peril, a natural counterweight to reckless abuse of policy. The only difference between a coercive state and a consortium of leading citizens is competence.

In the economic crisis that brought Hitler to power, leading citizens refused to participate. They stupidly entrusted the mechanism of state to Hindenburg, Hoover, and Chamberlain, who preferred National Socialism to Marxism. It is no surprise that German democracy ended badly in 1933. Politicians routinely proffer disaster, since their social contribution consists of flattery, fantasy, hatred and fear.

If roads are needed, communities have local bankers, landlords, and employers to determine and pay for local development. Ditto schools and hospitals. Every example of American philanthropy was an Andrew Carnegie or Sam Walton "rags-to-riches" story. My proposal is very simple. Do not let these men (or anyone else) compel obedience via legislation. Make the law of society de jure anarchy and promulgate the idea that some will govern more than others, not by virtue of piecrust campaign promises and balloon drops at a party meeting, but as a consequence of diligence, effort, savings, and sobriety.

It is silly to cry "fascism!" as an objection to my proposal. The operative feature of fascism was direction of industry by government. I hope that my critics have enough sense to say that an elite banking consortium constitutes an oligarchy, i.e., rule by a few, and is hence undemocratic. Quite so. Democracy is a disaster. Nothing you can say will convince me that your vote is equal to mine, or that the two of us together have a legal right to silence one of our economic or intellectual betters, or that someone's childish whims deserve to be given a free microphone in aid of "the public good."

I am not in favor of free speech. Nor do I believe that free speech exists in contemporary society. Speech is the weapon of broadcasters. These are trifling side issues, but it won't hurt to sweep them aside. I am a media exile. My works don't have a hope in hell of publication. As far as I'm concerned, CBS is a predatory force and their New York headquarters should be short-listed for a surgical strike.

The society in which we live is neither democratic nor fair. Take away their Federal license to print money, and CBS falls tomorrow. We cannot be rid of them too soon. Their agenda of glib vacuuity, opinion polls, blandishments, and flashy manure is anesthetizing our society. Sport is next on my hit list. If I were a religious man, I'd fall on my knees and beg God to turn the NFL into thirty pillars of salt, ending one of the vainest vulgarities in human history.

I hope I have demonstrated a core proposition, that your vote and mine are incompatible and cancel one another. If you comfort yourself with the knowledge that a "majority" agree with your preference, I hereby denounce your brainless majority as defacto fascism and blame you for wrecking the American economy. 44% of

GDP is government outlays [Federal, state and local]. When the stock market crashes, don't look for oligarchic villains on Wall Street, or State Street, or in Grand Cayman. The next Great Depression (see note) will be of your own majoritarian making, because you pretended that political wishes were horses and beggars could ride, if enough of them wanted to.

Ayn Rand had the right idea. The guiltiest of men are the natural oligarchs, who abdicated their leadership of an anarcho-capitalist revolution. Instead of giving Harry Truman the atomic bomb, it could have and should have been developed in a laboratory at Galt's Gulch. This is the moral meaning of inequality. When the men of brains collaborate with a mob of dullards, it's unfair to blame the resultant calamity on a crowd of pickpockets and cheerleaders. Sadly, a moral principle never reaches beyond itself. Its ethical arms are too short, extending no farther than one man's soul, one man's purpose and lifespan. We have to look elsewhere for political guidance, because the thing at issue is "a nation of laws and not of men."

I deal in very simple ideas. The rotten timber is a fiction, so let's blast the fictions. In reality, there are living human beings whose freedom and interest are the subject of this debate. There is no divine right of incorporation, whether as a government, or Subchapter S tax dodge, or a family trust that never dies like a natural person. I hereby propose that the law abolish all corporations. Let each parcel of land, each railroad and airline, every road and factory be the property of some individual (or partnership of individuals). Legal cases shall be A vs B, two natural persons. I don't care if embryos, animals, and plants qualify for legal standing. Fine. Whatever. But no more fictitious, disembodied, immortal "corporate persons" like the United States of America or CBS Inc. Let's get the bullshit out of the way and call some real defendants in court, to explain their guilt or innocence.

—

This essay was written in 1998, ten years before the Wall Street crash of 2008. During the past 16 years, Workforce Participation rate fell from 67% to 63%. Government debt (federal, state and local) nearly quadrupled, from $6 trillion to $21 trillion.

The Architecture of Liberal Democracy

Web published in 2005, cited by law journals in Asia

If someday in the distant future man is to rediscover the blessings of liberty, it will be helpful to have an architectural diagram. Pretty hard to build a stable structure without one.

I speak of it as liberal democracy because the term is traditional and it encapsulates nicely the goal of a free society. In a liberal democracy, anarchic institutions like an open market for goods and services (survival of the fittest) plus the discretionary (arbitrary and self-serving) powers of public officials are limited by the rule of law. A society is liberal only to the extent that liberty and equity are legally acknowledged and continually expanded, no matter what the Market or a triumphant political faction prefer to impose as expedient policy.

Perhaps my understanding of liberal democracy seems odd, since there no longer exists an example of free and equal society under law. The United States betrayed its legacy of liberty. Corporate graft, political horse trading, reckless military adventures, and paternal regulation of private conduct voided the U.S. Constitution repeatedly. All that remains today is democracy without much liberty, without common law, without recourse to equity or fixed principles of justice. Our courts no longer examine the merits of a case. They strictly apply statutes and precedents. Public officials and legislatures are deemed irresponsibly, unchallengeably sovereign. Individual Americans are no longer free and equal as a matter of right. Money talks, but nothing trumps pork barrel deficit spending and hand on heart bipartisan flagwaving.

Viewed from Africa, or Asia, or Europe, what happened in North America was simultaneously salutary and alarming. We rejoined the medieval world, where governments decide and citizens obey. The lamp of liberalism was snuffed out.

The Spirit of 76 became an imperial superpower and a brand identity, hypnotically flattering obese, incurious 'consumers of last resort.'

Fishing With Dynamite

It's easy to understand how the U.S. tragedy occurred of historical necessity. Men cannot grow a free, equal society with imported slaves and dispossessed, hostile Indian tribes. The American Experiment was conducted by and applied mainly to white Protestant colonists who settled the seaboard and galloped west. Inordinate anguish was the penalty, culminating in a Civil War that sundered Jeffersonian democracy at the price of a million casualties and five times the GNP in 1865, not including subsequent political graft and nine decades of Jim Crow segregation.

So we are compelled to consider theory, irrespective of the broken promise of American liberty and justice for all. The essential question is illuminated by a case in equity. Suppose that a neighbor, visitor, or stranger decides to go fishing with dynamite, instead of using hook and line. It's irrelevant whether he's rich or poor. Explosions and indiscriminate slaughter affect everyone living near the lake and deprive their children's children of fish stock. If one fellow is lazy and brazen enough to fish with dynamite to the obvious detriment of his neighbors and their innocent progeny, what grievous mayhem might be next?

The statist solution is legislation, regulation, licensing, fishing wardens, prosecutors, probation, prisons, and general taxation to pay for it all — none of which relies upon or makes use of equity jurisdiction. Shockingly similar to a juvenile delinquent fishing with dynamite, U.S. President Harry Truman ordered nuclear weapons dropped on civilian women and children (not military facilities) in Hiroshima and Nagasaki. It was undoubtedly indiscriminate mass murder of non-combatants, a war crime. Legislation, regulation, licensing, and taxation did not restrain or punish Truman — which Equity certainly would have.

So What Is This Equity Thing?

Originally an English chancery doctrine of righting wrongs, equity became a vital adjunct to American common law in colonial times. It persists today in probate, contract, family law and abatement of public nuisances (fishing with dynamite). The U.S. State of Georgia, for instance, codified Equity as a discretionary county court jurisdiction "established and allowed for the protection and relief of parties where, from any peculiar circumstances, the operation of general rules of law would be deficient in protecting from anticipated wrong or relieving for injuries done." The main equitable remedy is a restraining order, although equity can void contracts and compel action. If a dairy cow wanders away into a neighbor's farm, common law only allows the cow's owner to sue for money damages if his neighbor refuses to return the cow. An equity judge can order him to return the animal and jail him for contempt of court until he complies.

Equity jurisdiction is especially important for the protection of innocents. "Great inadequacy of consideration, joined with great disparity of mental ability in contracting a bargain, may justify equity in setting aside a sale or other contract." (Georgia 23-2-2) "In all cases of fraud, except fraud in the execution of a will, equity has concurrent jurisdiction with the law." (23-2-50) "Misrepresentation of a material fact, made willfully to deceive or recklessly without knowledge and acted on by the opposite party constitutes legal fraud." (23-2-52) "Any person who may not bring an action at law may complain in equity and every person who is remediless elsewhere may claim the protection and assistance of equity." (23-4-5) Traditional legal maxims of equity are simple and eloquent. Equity will not suffer a wrong to be without a remedy. Equality is equity. Equity regards substance rather than form. One who seeks equity must do equity. One who comes into equity must come with clean hands. Equity will not permit a party to profit by his own wrong. Equity delights to do justice and not by halves. Pretty swell, huh? But American equity is mostly inoperable.

Bad Doctrine, Insane Code

In a healthy society, Law is erected upon a balanced triangular base of The Market, Nature, and Ethics. Now consider what happens when 'wertfrei' market power (expressed in electoral ballots and campaign money) crowds out Nature and Ethics. Because no social order can stand on its head or on an inherently skittish random walk, an unrestrained market for ballots and campaign funds grows a new triangular base, the evil of which inevitably sprouts a rights-denying but law-like state Religion. In Nazi Germany, the religion was "Deutscheland Uber Alles." In Soviet Russia, Red China and postwar Labourite Britain, it was class consciousness. In postwar Israel and United States, preachers and sinners kneel obediently before a jealous supernatural God.

Actually, it's disingenuous to talk about "postwar" Israel and U.S., because their jointly operated god urged them to wage war more or less continually since 1947 to secure possession of The Holy Land, which somehow includes all of the oil fields in a 1000-mile radius of Jerusalem.

Our war in Iraq illustrates the progress of democracy unlimited by the rule of law, devoid of respect for human nature or ethics. In the aftermath of 9/11, hysterical Fear of the Other plus fear of change (Inertia) and plain Texan graft combined to interpret God's will for the people of Iraq to enhance the defense of Israel. I think Jehovah is planning something similar for Iran and Syria.

The environmental damage done by warfare in Iraq is difficult to exaggerate. 100,000 civilian war dead and maybe 75,000 seriously injured. U.N. staff estimated that 500,000 Iraqi children died during a decade-long U.S. blockade. Millions of rounds of depleted uranium are littered in every neighborhood in every Iraqi city, and there is no end in sight to "asymmetrical war," perhaps for a decade or more, until destruction and official conceit become so painful that Nature and Ethics are re-invited to share power, just like our Vietnam disaster a generation ago.

With so many Baby Boomers voting their ballots and wallets, it seems strange that Inertia and Fear of the Other blanked-out their know-ledge of what happened in Vietnam. Apparently, the Boomers were 'born again' by Graft in the 90s. If it's good for Wall Street and the Naz, that's all I need to know because I like being rich. Not much of a religious creed, but enough to shut everybody up at a White House prayer breakfast. Bill Clinton was particularly observant in worship of Israel's god, but George Bush has set some sort of record among U.S. presidents with his neurotic obsessive-compulsive nightly Bible readings in bed at precisely 8:45 pm.

How in Hell did this Trainwreck Happen?

The social influence of Law was eclipsed by Fear, Inertia, and Graft on numerous occasions in U.S. history. Mugler v Kansas was not unique among catastrophic Supreme Court precedents, but its scope has particular significance today in the context of an undefinable and unending Global War on Terror and heavy-handed Homeland Security.

> 'Government may require each citizen to so conduct himself, and so use his own property, as not unnecessarily to injure another.' But by whom, or by what authority, is it to be determined [what] will injuriously affect the public? Power to determine such questions, so as to bind all, must exist somewhere... Under our system that power is lodged with the legis-lative branch of the government. It belongs to that department to exert what are known as the police powers of the state, and to determine, primarily, what measures are appropriate or needful for the protection of the public morals, the public health, or the public safety. (123 U.S. 623)

This legitimated over a century of Congressional whimsy, panic and grandstanding. Post-9/11, U.S. lawmaking became little more than Inertia and Graft freighted with Fear. If the Republican majority enact a fascist police state, it will be U.S. Code, exempt from review by the courts. Your post-9/11 Bill of Rights and due process of law are already toast. That's why physically stressful interrogations, rendi-tion for torture by secret police, and perpetual detention with no presumption of innocence, no right to fair trial by jury, no right to confront your accusers, and no right to counsel of one's own choosing are deemed lawful Executive orders — so long as Congress averts a majority of blind frightened ayes of assent.

A healthy society could arise from the ashes of this terminal U.S. constitutional disaster, perhaps decades in the future, depending on the perspicacity of future American students of history and their ability to discriminate signal from noise on the web. I'm an optimist, so here goes.

Starting From Scratch

Rationality imposes the burden of evidence and an unencumbered commitment to discover and verify the pertinent facts. In the absence of conclusive evidence, the crush of exigency impels us to weigh scraps of data and make reasonable estimates and inferences. Bush and Blair turned this upside down, inventing and twisting scraps of lies at their leisure to cover up their covert purpose for invading Iraq (oil supplies for Israel, suppression of militant Arab resistance). Rational foreign policy requires exactly the reverse, an integration of available evidence without prejudice or covert agenda — a candid, unbiased, honest debate.

Issues that divide men cry out for creative thinking and thinking afresh, addressing The Unknown as well as the frozen contests between A and B, whose warring creeds and enmity are set in weathered limestone.

To kickstart a fresh perspective, let's ask: "Who is John Galt?" — the uncompromising liberator who can stop the motor of false government and free its most dutiful and culpable victims. (Evil requires the sanction of the victim.) The implicit conclusion is obvious, that all men and women of self-made soul, including you and I, should try to fill Galt's shoes. History smiled on simpletons like Boris Yeltsin and George Washington, so let's not disqualify anyone from inching along the revolution. The next child born might be Dagny II or Rearden XIV.

The foregoing was probably as clear as mud to some readers, especially those unfamiliar with Ayn Rand's novel Atlas Shrugged. Personally, I advise folks to skip backward in her body of work and read The Fountainhead instead — a much richer story of heroism, assuming that moral heroism blows your skirt up. If you are not excited by visions of independence there's not much else to discuss, because freedom is the whole of our future.

The long progress of human history was a steady erosion of authority. Monarchs, aristocrats, popes, fascists, and communists are kaput and entirely discredited as "liberators." They still exist, obviously, and billions of faithful serfs continue to sanction Leaders to absolve themselves of individual responsibility.

But an unconquered minority of thoughtful men and women worldwide won't wear chains for anybody. For these best and bravest, liberty and justice are the essential purpose of political struggle. The thing being struggled with is the Not Yet, Highly Unlikely, and Untested. That's what frightens people. It's nerve wracking and dangerous to experiment with our children firsthand, so cowards consign them to state educators and psychologists. The familiar hymns of Empire and Salvation are sung on every channel, every holiday, every workday. Custom is a steamroller monopoly of habit. Leaders brook little dissent, there is no Plan B, and consumers can't opt out. Probing outside the gulag of mainstream general consent is generally verboten.

The Bottom Line

If we can learn anything from Murray Rothbard or Robert Nozick, I believe it amounts to this: Don't work for a university or debate the utility of minarchist nightwatchmen. Don't argue for NAP or ZAP or natural law.

What's needed is a big dose of heroism, to explore the Unknown.

National Defense

posted at Anti-State.Com, 2003

Please read carefully and patiently. It sounds horrible because I have to use hot-button terms, like 'taxes' and 'governance,' which I hope you will weigh afresh without prejudice. To tax is simply to burden, like a surcharge for shipping and handling, or insured delivery, and that's all it means in the following scheme of governance.

First, I would stipulate many independent and competitive security agencies, not one monolithic "government." Lawyers will organize dispute settlement and other services that legitimize by their reasonableness numerous private security companies and *one* national defense company — a territorial utility with a natural monopoly. I think this is arguably a free market economic guesstimate of what will happen in the long run.

Private security companies will be local or specialized (in cyberspace grids, for instance) and supported voluntarily by their subscribers. If a security company goes bad, others can woo their disgruntled customers, much like airlines who open new routes of transport when they perceive fresh demand for a better, cheaper service. How to finance the monopoly national defense company (let's call it the Territorial Executive) is a thrawn conundrum with no good solution except taxation. How to levy and collect this tax is a core problem.

To my mind, the Territorial Executive should be an uniquely public corporation — the only one permitted in law with an impersonal, perpetual charter, which confers no domestic or civil police power but is legally competent to provide national territorial defense at the borders. Its shares would be publically traded, mostly held by its founding institutional subscribers (banks, pension funds, insurance companies) and their successors with deep pockets. Big players have most to lose if attacked or invaded.

Assuming that it's a small standing army, enough to patrol the shores and skies with a large, part-time volunteer reserve force, then taxes could be reasonably small. The hard question, I repeat, is how to levy and collect those national defense taxes. Voluntary payment of tax is not a credible solution, because of the free rider problem. Nor do I propose that taxes be collected by force or punitive legal process. Under the Freeman's Constitution, forcible imposition of tax is a crime against humanity.

Twenty years ago in *USA Inc* I proposed that national defense costs be apportioned among the 50 states, plus a head tax – say $100 a year per adult citizen. The math was okay, but it is an inoperative concept in pure ancap. We also need to imagine that there are many regions and communities not unlike, but far more numerous, than the 13 post-colonial American states under the Articles of Confederation, jealous and suspicious of each other. It is unlikely that 100 city-states and 5,000 rural districts will pay national defense taxes without grumbling, foot-dragging, and acrimony ("We're paying too much based on our population, or property value, which has declined, compared to so-and-so.") Ancap security firms will be similar in attitude to the customers and local communities they serve. Abide by court decisions? — yes, with considerable grumbling about legal fees. Cheerfully pay national defense taxes? — no.

So, I think that shareholders of this unique national defense corporation are going to end up holding the financial bag, which means that they will have to pass along an annual "rights cash call" (a levy on shares) to their customers and counterparties in the form of higher prices, maybe 1-2% of GDP. If someone gets tired of collecting taxes as a shareholder, they could sell to another company or a successful speculator (think George Soros or Ted Turner) who wants to exercise voting rights in National Defense Inc. and qualify as a shareholder for possible nomination and election as a director.

After a long and successful career in business, great men are not unnaturally drawn to politics and statesmanship. In the manner which I have described it, they can buy a vote by making big annual cash contributions to national defense. No man is likely to corner the market and become a tyrant, for the same reason that all historical attempts to hold a commodity to ransom (like the Hunt brothers making vast silver buys) have failed and must always fail. Many, many persons and financial institutions will want a piece of the Territorial Executive, and every newspaper on earth will be watching its every tick of share price. Berkshire Hathaway is a good metaphor for the Territorial Executive, with a market cap of $113 billion (1/3 privately held by Warren Buffett) and its share price in the stratosphere, currently $73,500 per share. See Note 1, below.

—

NOTE 1. Berkshire Hathaway Inc. is a holding company owning subsidiaries engaged in a number of diverse business activities, the most important of which are insurance businesses conducted on both a primary basis and a reinsurance basis. Berkshire's principal insurance businesses are GEICO, General Re, Berkshire Hathaway Reinsurance Group and Berkshire Hathaway Primary Group. Berkshire also owns and operates a number of other businesses that offer apparel, building products, finance and financial products and flight services.

NOTE 2. There is ample historical American precedent for businessmen funding national security. See http://www.robert-morris.com

NOTE 3. In previous writing ("The End of Fukuyama") I said: "We do not need a public treasury to provide for national defense or domestic tranquility. In point of legal fact, the U.S. government is bankrupt, and it is laughable to hear anyone speak of repaying the national debt. When this becomes irrefutably obvious in 2015, I suggest that we privatize the U.S. military-industrial complex, rather than remain its tax slaves. I don't see the point of forbidding foreign ownership, since U.S. policy is driven by Israel and the Security Council, cordially treating Russia and China as equals in a balance of power. Let's talk IPO. Give the Pentagon to Merrill Lynch and let them syndicate World Cop Inc. I'm sure that Britain, Germany, Japan, and New England [PADD 1] will buy a piece, to keep crude flowing northward from the slave-states of OPEC."

OTHER BOOKS BY WOLF DEVOON

Mars Shall Thunder
ISBN 978-1435714656

The Good Walk Alone
ISBN 978-1499595017

Laissez Faire Law
ISBN 978-1430308362

First Feature
ISBN 978-1430310150